MAURICE COLLIS was born in Ireland in 1889 and educated at Rugby and at Corpus Christi College, Oxford. Although his real ambition was to be a writer, he entered the Indian Civil Service and went to Burma, where he served in various administrative and secretarial appointments for 23 years. In 1936 he retired from the Civil Service and immediately began his literary career. Since that time he has published an impressive list of books including histories, plays, novels, art and literary criticism. Maurice Collis is well known in this country as the author of FOREIGN MUD, THE LAND OF THE GREAT IMAGE, THE QUEST FOR SITA, and THE FIRST HOLY ONE.

CORTÉS AND MONTEZUMA

MAURICE COLLIS

A DISCUS BOOK/PUBLISHED BY AVON BOOKS

AVON BOOKS
A division of
The Hearst Corporation
959 Eighth Avenue
New York, New York 10019

First Discus Printing, September, 1978

DISCUS TRADEMARK REG. U.S. PAT. OFF. AND IN
OTHER COUNTRIES, MARCA REGISTRADA, HECHO EN
U.S.A.

Printed in the U.S.A.

To
Viscount Astor
with warm regards

Contents

Contents

CORTÉS AND MONTEZUMA

Montezuma is shown seated on a mat
on his throne. His head-dress is the
crown of Mexico. Above his head is
the phonetic rebus of his name

Maps

Introduction

The Portuguese, by their discoveries and conquests east of the Red Sea in the sixteenth century, were the people who brought Europe and Asia together in modern times. While they were going East, the Spaniards were going West. In the Spanish conquest of Mexico the clash between the Catholic thought of Europe and the system of ideas which prevailed in Central America was more violent than the clash between European and Asian thought. The Portuguese made little immediate impression on India, but the Spanish way of life quickly prevailed in America. I had found it a subject of great interest to trace the interaction of the cultures of Europe and the Orient. The clash in the opposite direction, when I came to study it, seemed yet more absorbing, because it was concentrated in a single event of an extraordinary kind, the meeting of Cortés with Montezuma. The facts of the drama in which these two men were involved are, in general, well established. Prescott, in the nineteenth century, and Madariaga in recent years, have covered the ground in long scholarly books. But what the facts mean remains, and perhaps will always remain, in dispute. For Prescott the hero was Cortés, a white adventurer who achieved with a handful of men the conquest of a powerful barbarian kingdom. Madariaga, aware that this was an old-fashioned simplification in view of the extensive information which is becoming available about the ancient and curious civilization of Central America, presented Cortés in a more modern historical perspective. He remains, however, the leading figure of the drama.

The present book, hardly as much as a quarter as long as Prescott's or Madariaga's, is an attempt to interpret the facts

Introduction

in the light of the latest researches into the Mexican way of thought. My first concern has been to try for a clear and consistent explanation of each situation as it arrives. Without intending disrespect to what is an historical classic, one is obliged to say that Prescott in his *The Conquest of Mexico* fails to make sense of many of the singular events which he describes. It was, indeed, impossible for any writer to do so in the period when he wrote. Madariaga in his *Hernán Cortés*, acutely conscious that Prescott does not make sense, strives to do so with all the learning at his command. I have struggled to take Madariaga's elucidations a little further. In this difficult task I have been greatly·helped by advice given me by Mr. C. A. Burland, the eminent student of Central America's old magical books, whose kindness and generosity are no less noteworthy than his scholarship. As I worked on the sources I came to see Montezuma as an even stranger personage than has generally been supposed. He cannot, as in former books, be given second place. The drama is his as much as Cortés'. Indeed, of the two protagonists he is the more interesting because he is the more mysterious. To penetrate the mystery of his actions is one of the chief objects of this book.

For those already acquainted with the subject, I should state that I have not used the term 'Aztec', hitherto employed to denominate the race which ruled Central America at the time of the conquest. The race was called the Mexica in its own language, Nauatl. The Spanish writers contemporary with the conquest use this word in its form as Mexican. 'Aztec' is not found in the Nauatl language. It was coined by Europeans after the conquest and seems to be of questionable validity. The time has come to forget it. The time has also come, I think, to discontinue the term 'Indians' for the original Americans. But that will be more difficult.

The spelling of all the Mexican names and their translations are taken from the index and glossary of Vol. II of the *Codex Mendoza* as edited by James Cooper Clark.

Introduction

The authorities I have used are cited in the text, though page references are omitted as being unsuitable for an essay of this kind. The student, however, will have no difficulty in locating them. I am indebted to Mr. Nicholas Egon for helping me with Dr. Seler's German translation of Sahagún's Nauatl text, to Mr. Cawthra Mulock who lent me a suggestive article on on the cosmic aspects of Mexican mythology, and to Dr. Joseph Needham who drew my attention to Jacques Soustrelle's *La Pensée Cosmologique des Anciens Mexicains*.

The quotations from authorities are in inverted commas, but in some passages (for instance, Bernal Díaz's soliloquy on the old Conquistadors at the end of the book) inverted commas are not used, because the passages are not direct quotations, but rather the summary of the text.

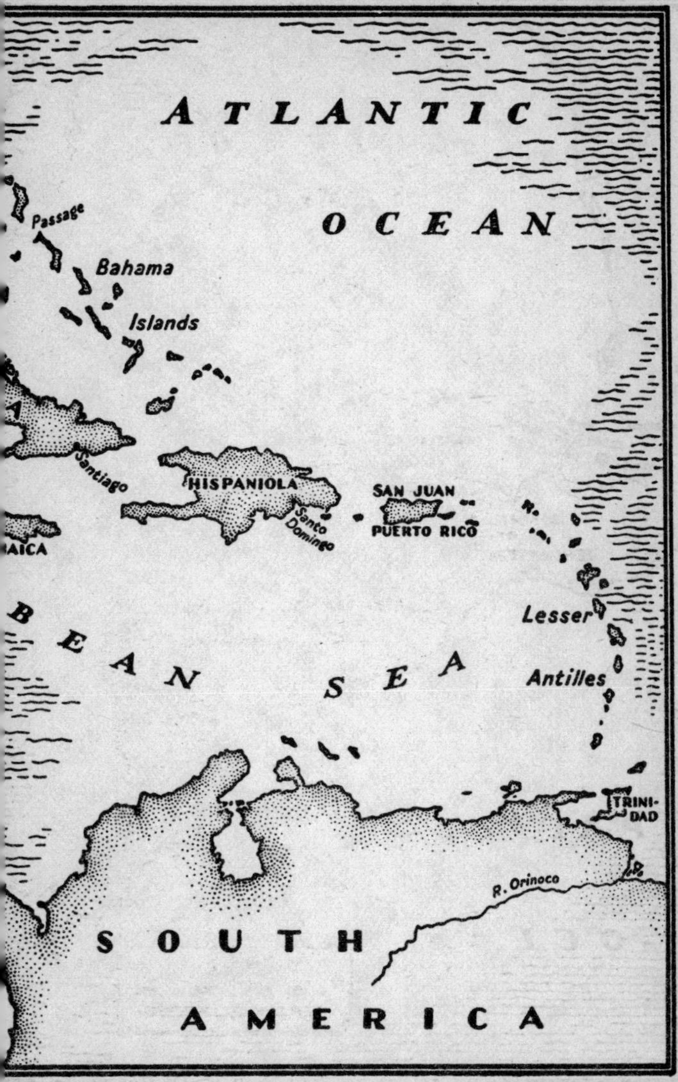

ATLANTIC
OCEAN
Passage
Bahama
Islands
Santiago
HISPANIOLA
Santo Domingo
SAN JUAN
PUERTO RICO
AICA
Lesser
Antilles
BEAN SEA
TRINI-DAD
R. Orinoco
SOUTH
AMERICA

𝕮 I 𝕭

Cortés in the West Indies

The Magnificent Lord Cristóbal Colón (whom we always call Christopher Columbus) sighted Watling Island in the Bahamas on 11th October 1492. Thence he went on to discover the West Indian islands of Cuba and Hispaniola (Haiti). On his return to Spain in 1493, he informed King Ferdinand that he had reached the outlying parts of eastern Asia, somewhere in the neighbourhood of Japan or China. He did not know that the continent of America lay between what he had discovered and what he thought he had discovered.

The two kingdoms of the Iberian peninsula, Spain and Portugal, were exploring in opposite directions. When Columbus discovered the West Indies, the Portuguese were navigating as far as the Cape of Good Hope in a methodical attempt to reach the East Indies. To avoid disputes in the future the two countries asked the Borgia Pope, Alexander VI, to demarcate their spheres of interest. Taking a pen he drew a line down the middle of the Atlantic and in a Bull called *Inter Caetera* declared the Portuguese to have exclusive rights to all lands they already possessed or might discover eastward of it and the Spaniards a similar right to what Columbus had discovered in the West Indies and to what subsequently they might come upon beyond those islands.

In this way the Spaniards were presented with the American

mainland before they knew of its existence. Its discovery was a gradual process. Six years passed before Columbus, during his third voyage to the West Indies, sighted a piece of it. In August 1498 he came upon the north coast of South America near the mouth of the Orinoco river. The coast westwards from the Orinoco to the isthmus of Darien was explored between 1498 and 1502 by Vespucci. Cabot also landed in Florida and Cabral in Brazil. In all these places the Spaniards found only jungles and savages. There was little or no sign of gold, the acquisition of which was their principal object. They were also much in the dark as to what they had discovered. As yet they did not know of the Pacific Ocean.

In 1508 an attempt was made to settle on the coast of Colombia in South America, but it failed. Five years later, in September 1513, Balboa caught sight of the Pacific from a peak in Darien, the great occasion which was afterwards to inspire Keats in his famous sonnet—'Much have I travelled in the realms of gold'—though he thought it was 'stout Cortés' (not Balboa) who 'with eagle eyes stared at the Pacific'. Balboa descended from the peak and in full armour waded into the new ocean, which he took possession of in the name of the King of Spain. Soon afterwards a settlement was founded in Darien near the present Panama Canal.

Meanwhile, the Spaniards had been organizing their first discovery, the West Indies. The island of Hispaniola or Little Spain was the first to be settled. Adventurers of all classes sailed across the Atlantic, hoping to get rich quick. Some were granted estates and labour to work them. The labourers were the unfortunate inhabitants, who before the arrival of the Spaniards had been living a carefree life under their chiefs. They were amiable, happy peoples, rather like South Sea Islanders. Reduced to the condition of serfs, made to work hard on the plantations and at washing for gold, and very cruelly treated besides, they lost heart and died in great numbers.

Among the adventurers who came out was Hernán Cortés.

He arrived in Hispaniola in 1504, aged nineteen. His father was a country gentleman of Extremadura and had sent him at fourteen to Salamanca University to study law. He stayed there awhile, but left without taking his degree. An outdoor life was what he wanted. He thought at first of a military career in Italy, but decided to go to the West Indies. His father gave him the money for the voyage and he sailed for what was still thought to be an outlying part of India or China.

He had introductions to some of the government people at Santo Domingo, the principal Spanish town in Hispaniola, and after a while was given an estate with serf labour. For the next seven years he remained on the island working his lands. Nothing much is known about him at this period, except that he was made Public Notary of Azúa, a small town near Santo Domingo, being qualified for such a post on account of his legal studies.

In 1511, at the age of twenty-six, he joined the expedition of Diego Velázquez, who was ordered by the Viceroy of the Indies, Columbus's son, to subdue the great neighbouring island of Cuba, in which as yet there was no Spanish settlement. The conquest was easy, as the inhabitants were too terrified of the Spaniards to make a stubborn resistance. After the campaign, Cortés was appointed Velázquez's chief secretary. He remained in Cuba for eight years and became one of the most well-to-do landlords in the island. During these years he took no part in the voyages of exploration which were gradually revealing the coastline of the American continent. As a result of two of these voyages, which will be described in the next chapter, the empire of Mexico was located, a country whose inhabitants were observed to be civilized, unlike the tribesmen with whom the Spaniards had hitherto come in contact. As of the seven years Cortés lived in Hispaniola, so now of his eight years in Cuba, we know little. He married a Spanish woman called Catalina Xuárez, he fell foul of the Governor, Diego Velázquez, and was reconciled to him, and he became Magistrate of the chief town, Santiago. In all this there was nothing to suggest that he was soon to emerge as the dominating personality of that region. His friends may have guessed he had great capacity, but none of them put it in writing at that date. Had they done so, it could only have been an opinion; for as yet he had had no opportunity of displaying the extraordinary nature of his talents. His character was independent, his manner charming, he was bold and clever, but that he was a military genius and a great man of affairs, subtle and far-seeing, cannot have occurred even to his most intelligent companions. Yet possessing as he certainly did such latent powers, was he himself unaware of them? One must suppose not. How then was he content to remain for fifteen years in the little world of Cuba doing little more than amuse and enrich himself? One can only surmise he was awaiting his opportunity. Before he could have scope, he must have an independent command. As will be seen, the discovery of Mexico was his opportunity. When it came, he recognized it as his hour and resolved that he would conquer Mexico, though the prospect was one of appalling difficulty and danger.

ᘓ2ᘐ

The Discovery of Mexico

Diego Velázquez was a handsome, rather stout man, well off and easy going. As the subordinate of the Viceroy of the Indies, he was not free to discover new lands and settle them himself without reference to his superior. If he made a discovery, he had to report it, when the Viceroy or the King of Spain could appoint him its ruler or, if they pleased, give the appointment to someone else. Velázquez, however, believed that if he made a worthwhile discovery, he had enough interest at the Court of Spain to keep it for himself.

In January 1517 a certain Hernández de Córdoba came to see him, accompanied by a hundred and ten young Spanish residents of Cuba. Córdoba was a rich man with a big estate, but the rest had not had lands allotted to them and were soldiers of fortune, who were anxious to go further afield and find some place where they might settle and grow rich. Among them was Bernal Díaz del Castillo, a needy young gentleman of twenty-five, who when an old man wrote *The True History of the Conquest of New Spain*, the most delightful, detailed and reliable of all the books written about Cortés and the conquest of Mexico. Córdoba explained to Velázquez that his companions had elected him their captain and that he was ready to put up money for a voyage of discovery, if Velázquez would authorize it and make a contribution. An agreement was reached: Velázquez promised to provide one ship and provisions, if Córdoba supplied two ships.

The expedition left Cuba in February 1517. The course set was West. The central American mainland which had so far been discovered (and had been disappointingly poor and savage) lay southwards of the islands. The explorers had therefore no idea what, if anything, they would come upon to the westward. 'Trusting to luck,' writes Bernal Díaz, 'we steered towards the setting sun, knowing nothing of the depth of water, nor of the currents, nor of the winds that usually prevail in that latitude.'

The west point of Cuba is only 150 miles from the top of Yucatán, the thick peninsula which forms the southern arm of the Bay of Mexico. But the Spaniards did not know this and when, after surviving a dangerous storm, they descried Catoche, its northern cape, they were relieved, though of course they could not tell whether the place was an island or part of the mainland. On coming close in, they saw in the distance a large town, and were astonished to perceive that many of its buildings were of stone, which was never used by the native inhabitants of the West Indies or the mainland further south. It must be a rich place they thought. There might be gold there.

What they had actually discovered was one of the civilized races of America, the Maya, a people who from the fourth century A.D. had developed a high culture. They were the greatest astronomers and mathematicians in the world of their time. As architects, potters, painters and sculptors, they had produced many great works of art. And they had developed a picture writing. They lived in large and beautiful stone cities. But Córdoba and his men saw nothing of this.

Bernal Díaz has described what they did see. When the ships were anchored off shore, ten large canoes put out full of men. The Spaniards beckoned to them to come aboard. About thirty of them did so. They were clothed in cotton jackets and loin-cloths. It was impossible to converse with them except by signs. But they seemed very cheerful and friendly. A string of green beads was given to each one. On leaving they intimated that they would return next day, take the Spaniards ashore, and let them have water and provisions. They returned as promised. The hundred-odd Spaniards landed in their own boats, taking their arms as a precaution. Fifteen of them were crossbowmen and ten musketeers. The beach was crowded with a multitude of spectators. A man, who appeared to be the governor of the place, received the visitors. His expression and gestures denoted, apparently, the utmost goodwill as he invited them to the town, which was a few miles distant. Marching in a compact body, the Spaniards set out with him. He led them, however, into an ambush. Suddenly they were attacked with great fury by a large force of soldiers in quilted armour, who discharged arrows, stones from slings, and javelins by means of throwing sticks. In the first few moments fifteen Spaniards were wounded, but the main body stood firm, fired their muskets and crossbows, and used their steel swords, weapons superior to any carried by the enemy. The Maya soldiers, who had never seen fire-arms, crossbows, or steel, lost their nerve and ran, leaving fifteen dead and two prisoners.

Nearby was a courtyard and three houses of masonry, which were found to be oratories and to contain images of gods. These sculptures seemed very hideous to the Spaniards, who could not appreciate an art which was different from that of the Renaissance. Moreover, since it was an art devoted to a religion alien to theirs, they were the further prejudiced. Indeed, not until quite recently have Europeans been able to admire pre-Columbian American art. But what Córdoba and his men could admire were things they found in some boxes in the temple—golden necklaces and diadems, and fish and ducks of gold. These they took and hurriedly retreated to their ships.

After the wounded were bandaged, the party decided to continue westwards and explore the Yucatán coast. They had made a wonderful discovery, though the glimpse of it had been tantalizingly short. Perhaps they would have better luck further on. Their two prisoners were taught some Spanish, so as to become interpreters. After a while the coast turned south-west. Days passed and, when the drinking water was very low, another large town was sighted, known afterwards as Campeche. There the Spaniards had an experience, which it was difficult to make sense of. Going ashore with their water casks, they filled them at a pool near the town. Hardly was this done when some Mayas of the upper class, dressed in smart cotton mantles, approached and asked by signs whether they came from the sunrise, repeating several times a word which sounded like 'Castilan'. On the Spaniards saying they came from that quarter, the Mayas invited them to enter the town. After their experiences at Catoche they hesitated, but, on talking it over, decided to go. They were taken straight to a large stone building which was evidently a temple. The interior was frescoed with pictures of deities and large serpents. In the centre was an altar covered with fresh blood, as if sacrifices had just been made on it. The Spaniards were disturbed by the sight of the altar, though many women moved laughing among them. Presently some men in ragged mantles, who looked like slaves, piled up reeds for a fire and two squadrons of archers drew up nearby. Then suddenly there emerged from an oratory to one side a number of sinister figures. They wore white cotton cloaks, reaching to their feet, their faces were painted black, and their long hair was matted with blood. These priests, for that is who they were, carried pottery braziers in which a copal incense was smoking. They approached the Spaniards and fumigated them, as a Catholic priest might incense a holy thing. Having done so, they drew attention to the prepared fire, lit it, and intimated that the Spaniards should leave before it went out. The archers, and other soldiers who had crowded near, now began to whistle and sound their drums in so threatening a manner that it was deemed prudent to return immediately to the ships.

The meaning of this encounter was not understood by the

Spaniards until they became better acquainted with that part of the world.

Fifty miles further down the Yucatán coast the voyagers came in sight of Chanpoton. A river flowed into the sea three miles from this large town and they thought the water casks could be filled there without attracting much attention. But they rashly stayed the night on land and at dawn found themselves surrounded by Maya troops who outnumbered them two hundred to one. A fierce battle followed in which the Spaniards lost fifty men killed. The remaining fifty or so, all wounded, some desperately, regained the ships with the greatest difficulty, having to abandon their casks. There was nothing to be done but return to Cuba. Soon after reaching it, Córdoba died of his wounds. It was a catastrophe.

However, Velázquez, the Governor, was much impressed by the news they brought of a civilization in advance of any met with since Columbus had discovered the Indies. The sight of the gold ornaments taken at Catoche delighted him. He decided to send another expedition. This left in April of the following year, 1518, under the command of Juan de Grijalva, a relative of his. Velázquez provided a larger share in the expenses than on the previous occasion, but the provisions were paid for by some young landowners of distinction who joined the expedition. Altogether 240 Spaniards went, each bringing his own arms, among them Bernal Díaz del Castillo again, this time with the rank of ensign. Velázquez told them to take the same route as Córdoba and go beyond Chanpoton, his furthest point. If feasible they should make a settlement. Above all they should try to get gold, either by barter or seizure. After they left, he wrote off to his friends at the Court of Spain to inform them of his discovery of a new rich country and to ask them to work for his appointment as its Governor. In this he was intriguing behind the back of his superior, the Viceroy of the Indies, who claimed the right of adding to his existing jurisdiction whatever discoveries his subordinates might make. It is necessary to note this manœuvre, because later it suggested to Cortés how to go over Velázquez's head and appeal direct to Charles, nephew of Ferdinand, who in 1518 had become King of Spain at the age of eighteen.

Grijalva and his 240 companions failed to make Cape Catoche and were carried south by currents to the island of Cozumel, a short distance down the east coast of Yucatán. On seeing the ships the islanders fled. Failing to induce them to return, Grijalva left and, passing Catoche and Campeche without landing, arrived at Chanpoton where Córdoba had met with disaster. The Spaniards had more fire-arms on this occasion and going ashore drove off the Maya soldiers who resisted them. After staying three days in the town, which was deserted and where they could find no gold, they continued their voyage along the coast. At Tabasco, a coastal area between the Maya country and Mexico, they managed, with the help of the two Maya captives taken by Córdoba who were by now able to interpret a little, to persuade the inhabitants to barter gold for coloured glass beads; glass, not being known in America, was mistaken for jade, a stone which was much prized. Continuing westwards along the coast, they passed without knowing it the Mexican border. The landscape changed; it became more mountainous and they beheld far inland a great snow peak, an astonishing spectacle in the sweltering heat of June in the tropics. (This was the volcano of Orizaba [18,700 feet] behind which on a plateau, 7,000 feet high, stood the fabulous city of Mexico.)

Soon they were to have a curious experience. At the mouth of a river about fifty miles short of the future Vera Cruz they saw a number of people carrying white flags on long poles, which they waved to the ships, as if inviting them to stop. An armed party was sent ashore to investigate. On return they reported to Grijalva that they had found some well-dressed men seated in the shade with mats before them, on which were spread fruit, fowls and maize cakes. The Spaniards were invited by signs to sit down and eat. As their hosts did not speak the Maya language, the interpreters were useless. Censers were brought and the Spaniards were fumigated.

On hearing this report, Grijalva went ashore himself. He was received with the greatest respect. After distributing some of his glass beads, he managed to make it understood that he would give more, if they brought him gold. This they did and during the next few days the Spaniards got in exchange for beads gold jewellery worth sixteen thousand pieces of eight. Owing to the language difficulty, Grijalva could not ascertain why he had been beckoned ashore and entertained, and who precisely his hosts were.

Later on, the full meaning of these events will be given. Suffice it at present to say that the men at the river mouth had been told by Montezuma, the King of Mexico, to watch for the Spaniards' arrival and invite them ashore. He had already been informed of Grijalva's landings at Chanpoton and Tabasco. He thought the strangers might be the people of the god Quetzalcoatl, whose return he was expecting. As this was a matter of the greatest importance for him and his kingdom, he had instructed the watchers to send him a full report in the Mexican picture writing.

Grijalva left the river and continued his voyage a little further westwards, sure that he had made a great discovery, overjoyed at the gold, but unable to find a clear explanation of what had happened. At the few places where he landed, nothing of note was observed, except that at an island he called San Juan de Ulúa he found the bodies of two boys who had just been sacrificed in a temple. Their bleeding hearts were in a receptacle below an image. This was his first glimpse of the Mexican religion, with which the Spaniards were afterwards to become so familiar.

It was now July and Grijalva decided to return to Cuba. He might have tried to settle, but thought it too risky. As he had no Mexican interpreter, he could not negotiate with the local lords. His two Maya interpreters must have known they had reached Mexico and told him so. They may also have known and told him that there was a great king living beyond the mountains. But that was all very vague. Accordingly he sent ahead his lieutenant, Pedro de Alvarado, one of the paladins of the future conquest, in the fastest sailer to tell Velázquez the news and deliver the gold, while he himself returned more slowly with the other three ships. They reached Cuba in November after an absence of seven months.

$\mathcal{E}3\mathcal{Z}$

Cortés Sets Out

The news of the discovery of Mexico, a country evidently much richer in gold than the West Indies, greatly delighted everyone in Cuba. Life in the island was pleasant enough for the Spaniards with estates, serf labour and gold washings. Yet, there was a shortage of labour, for the native inhabitants ran away, committed suicide or died of heart-break and overwork owing to the intolerable way they were treated. And the gold did not amount to much. So, to hear of a country where quantities of gold could be had in exchange for worthless beads was very attractive. For those with no estates, the news was of course more exciting still.

Since their arrival in the New World the Spaniards had seized by force everything they could. Their right to do so rested on the Borgia's Bull, which had given them America. Had they doubted their right to take other people's lands, their consciences would have been salved by the reflection that in bringing Christianity they were bringing salvation. Moreover, they were sure that the European way of life they introduced was superior to the native cultures they destroyed, as were afterwards the British in India or Africa. For all these reasons it was natural that they were in a fever to get all they could out of this wonderful new kingdom of Mexico.

But how to do it? The Spaniards in Cuba were very few in

numbers. Mexico was seemingly much stronger than any place they had gone against. A large population, stone towns, a great king in the mountains, well-armed forces. Such a prize was not easily to be had. That the most daring and adventurous spirits in the island believed that Cortés could conduct so difficult an enterprise with success is the explanation of his sudden rise to leadership at this time.

Bernal Díaz gives a portrait sketch of him, and though it was written after he had become a great figure, the parts of it I quote here describe him as he was in 1518. 'He was a tall man, well proportioned and robust. His face had little colour and was inclined to be greyish. His eyes were grave, though not without kindness. His hair and beard were black and rather thin. He had a deep chest and broad shoulders, was lean and slightly bow-legged. Both as a horseman and a swordsman he was very skilful. Above all he had courage and spirit, which is what matters most of all. As a youth in Hispaniola he was somewhat dissolute about women, and fought with knives several times with strong and agile men, and always won. There was a knife scar near his under lip and, if one looked hard at it, he was inclined to cover it up more with his beard. He was very affable to his companions, was a Latin scholar and something of a poet. Every morning he recited prayers from a Book of Hours and heard Mass with devoutness. He was fond of cards and dice and excessively fond of women.'

This lively and gallant young man was thirty-two years of age when Grijalva's messenger, Pedro de Alvarado, arrived with the great news about Mexico. 'Alvarado,' says Bernal Díaz, 'knew very well how to tell his story, and they say that Diego Velázquez could do nothing but embrace him, and order great rejoicings and sports for eight days.' Velázquez determined to send a new expedition, large enough this time to make a settlement. It would be impossible to keep the secret from the Viceregal court in Hispaniola, but the expedition could be represented to the authorities there as bent on no more than exploring the coast again. He would send another emissary to the Court of Spain, urging afresh that he be made Governor of the new lands and independent of Hispaniola. That would entitle him, under the prevailing custom, to a fifth of all the loot or profits, after the Royal Fifth had been paid. He would become an enormously rich man and in five years or so could return home with a good chance of a title and a high office at Court. But, as we shall see, Cortés thought otherwise. He determined that the fortune and the honours should be his.

To make sure of success, Velázquez ought to have led the expedition himself. But he was not a soldier and had no taste for hardships. The undertaking, he knew, was very hazardous. Better to send a trusted commander, who would do the hard work and run the risks, while he sat in Cuba and, if all went smoothly, reaped the reward. He must be prudent, too, about how much of his own money he put in. Quite a lot would be required, as the force needed would have to be bigger than on the two previous occasions. He would do well to chose as commander a man of means, able and ready to subscribe a substantial sum. With these requirements in mind, he turned for advice to his staff and the members of his household.

Various names were put forward. To begin with, there were three Velázquez relations who wanted the command. And why not Grijalva again? asked his companions of the late voyage, who liked him as a captain. But Cortés knew how to play the winning card. Velázquez had two favourites, his secretary and his accountant. Cortés made a bargain with them: 'Get me the command and you share in the proceeds.' They persuaded Velázquez against his better judgment, for though reconciled with Cortés and even the godfather of his daughter, he had not forgotten that some years before Cortés had tried to get the better of him. Nevertheless, when urged by his favourites, he appointed him. The written instructions Cortés received were framed so widely that, in effect, he had discretion to do whatever he thought best. Velázquez, however, arranged to send along with him some of his own partisans to keep him under observation.

Once in command, Cortés set to work to collect men and stores at Santiago, the capital. He made it quite clear that his object was more than exploration and barter. It was an expedition to conquer Mexico. The bait of so splendid and lucrative an adventure attracted the most resolute and daring men in Cuba. Says Bernal: 'He issued a proclamation that whoever went with him to the newly discovered lands to conquer them and settle there should receive his share of the gold, silver and riches, which might be gained.' To finance the venture, he mortgaged his estate for eight thousand gold pieces. At his request his friends sold their farms, bought weapons and horses, prepared cassava bread and salt pork and made quilted cotton armour. As there was no corn, cassava flour made of pounded manioc root had to serve. Quilted armour, suggested by those who had seen the Mayas using it, was made because there was not nearly enough steel armour to go round. Search was made for cannon, guns, powder and crossbows, and particularly for horses, which were very scarce. Neither Córdoba nor Grijalva had taken horses, but Cortés, having heard there were none in America, foresaw the enormous advantage which even a small troop of mailed cavalry would give him.

So the preparations went on. Cortés, as Bernal says, 'began to adorn himself and be more careful of his appearance, wearing a plume of feathers and a medal, a gold chain and a velvet cloak trimmed with knots of gold.' He had banners woven, on which, worked in gold, were the royal arms and a cross, with the legend: 'We shall conquer under the sign of the Cross.' These he set up in front of his house.

All this began to disquiet Velázquez. Could he be sure of Cortés? At the head of his force, when it was complete, Cortés would be the most powerful man in the island. If he could hardly be controlled in Cuba, how could he be controlled at all in Mexico? He might very well keep the conquest for himself. Perhaps it was not too late to revoke his appointment.

Cortés Sets Out

When Cortés heard rumours of this, he hastened his preparations, while he used all his charm to allay the Governor's suspicions. He used to show himself frequently at the palace and assure Velázquez how rich a man he would soon make him. It became clear, however, that the Governor, urged by his household to displace Cortés, was about to do so. Advised of this, Cortés, though his preparations were not complete, sent his force secretly on board the ships one night and sailed from Santiago the next morning.

There are two accounts of the final scene. Bernal says that Cortés, supported by his friends, called on Velázquez to say good-bye the evening before leaving, and that the next morning Velázquez was at the wharf to see him off, but on neither occasion came to the point of cancelling his commission. The other account is that there was no farewell on the eve of departure and Velázquez was entirely ignorant that Cortés was leaving. Hearing early in the morning that the fleet was about to sail, he rushed down to the harbour to stop it. Cortés was already on board his flagship, but seeing Velázquez on the wharf, he thought it best to take a boat and get within speaking distance. Velázquez reproached him for stealing away and Cortés replied over the intervening water that there were moments in life when it was necessary to act first and talk afterwards. Velázquez, being powerless to apprehend him, had to let him go. This lively story is preferred by some leading historians to Bernal's, but the objection to it is that while Bernal was on the spot, for he had joined the expedition, Las Casas, a Dominican friar, the author of the story, was not in Cuba at the time. I prefer Bernal's account also because it is truer to Cortés' character. His way was always to keep up appearances as long as possible. To have defied Velázquez at this stage would have been to put himself in the wrong and shocked at least some of his soldiers, who had no wish to be called rebels. Nor would Velázquez's partisans have sailed with him. It seems more likely, as Bernal suggests, that Cortés was clever enough to know, when he said good-bye to Velázquez, how by charm, flattery and loyal protestations to make him hesitate to revoke the appointment.

So Cortés got away from Santiago. But as he had not completed his preparations, he put into Trinidad, a town 350 miles further west along the Cuban coast. There he added substantially to his force. It was from the estates in this neighbourhood that the most famous of his paladins came to join him, Pedro de Alvarado with his brothers, and Juan de Escalante, Cristóbal de Olid, Alonso Puertocarrero and Gonzalo de Sandoval. These men, mostly between thirty and thirty-five, Cortés' age, were all of good birth. Of the rank and file we know nothing. But they were not mercenaries; they brought their own arms and equipment, and were rather a brotherhood of adventurers than soldiers in any modern sense. Yet, they were not like the buccaneers of a succeeding age, for they thought of themselves as the King of Spain's men and were to be scrupulous in laying aside for him his customary due, the Royal Fifth.

When Velázquez heard that Cortés was at Trinidad, he sent word to the chief magistrate there to detain and send him back to Santiago. It seems that he had at last made up his mind that he must take this drastic step, as he had become convinced that Cortés was setting off as an independent adventurer. But Cortés, surrounded by his brilliant staff, had no difficulty in talking over the chief magistrate. The answer sent back to Santiago was that Cortés spoke and acted as Velázquez's faithful servant, and that in any case it would be imprudent to meddle with him, for his soldiers might revenge him by sacking the town. And Cortés himself wrote a most loyal and flattering letter (which he could hardly have done had he broken with Velázquez in Santiago harbour).

After ten days the ships moved to Havana, a little further along the coast, where the local gentlemen received Cortés with acclamations and more hidalgos joined him. 'It was here in Havana,' says Bernal, 'that Cortés began to organize a Household and to be treated as a Lord.' Velázquez made one more attempt to prevent him from leaving, sending a yet more urgent demand for his arrest. But who was going to arrest the man whom everybody in Cuba now believed would enrich the island with the spoils of Mexico? Bernal sums it up: 'The Alvarados, Puertocarrero, Olid, Escalante, all of us would have given our lives for Cortés.'

When the expedition left Havana on 10th February 1519, it consisted of 11 ships, the largest being about a hundred tons,

	508 swordsmen
	100 sailors
	32 crossbowmen
	13 musketeers;
and carried	10 brass cannon
	4 small cannon
	16 horses

and a quantity of powder, ball, crossbow arrows and spare parts, and a number of dogs.

$\mathcal{E}4\mathcal{3}$

Cortés Arrives in Mexico

Cortés took the same course as had Grijalva. There is no need to describe the voyage in full, but certain events have to be mentioned.

It will be recalled that when Córdoba landed at Campeche on the western coast of Yucatán and met the Mayas on the beach, they asked whether he and his men came from the sunrise and repeated the word 'Castilan'. Though the explanation of this was not clear at the time, it was taken later to mean that the Mayas had seen Spaniards before. There was a rumour that some Spaniards, sailing from Darien in 1511, had been driven ashore on the east coast of the Yucatán isthmus. Like Grijalva's, Cortés' first port of call was Cozumel, the island that lies north-east on the isthmus. When there, it occurred to him to inquire whether any of these castaways were alive in the interior. He was informed by the local people that two were there. One called Aguilar eventually was found. He was bronzed the colour of a Maya and dressed like one. 'He had his hair shorn like a slave of those parts, carried a paddle on his shoulder, was shod with one old sandal, the other being attached to his belt, and had on a ragged old cloak and a worse loincloth. He had tied up in a bundle in his cloak a Book of Hours, old and worn.' Thus Bernal Díaz saw him. This Aguilar told a long story about the fate of his shipwrecked companions. Most of them had been sacrificed at the temples. Besides himself one other only was left alive, but he was happily married to a Maya wife and, though Aguilar urged him to join Cortés, he refused to leave her. Indeed, his sympathies were with the Mayas and he was said to have urged the Cape Catoche townsmen to attack Córdoba's men.

Aguilar turned out to be an important reinforcement for the expedition. He spoke the Maya language fluently. Of the two Mayas captured by Córdoba at Catoche, one was now interpreter with Cortés, but he was not reliable. Aguilar was in every way more suitable, although, as he did not speak Mexican, he would be of no use later on. But a happy chance at Tabasco was to provide Cortés with a way of getting over that difficulty.

Unlike Córdoba and Grijalva, Cortés did not land at Catoche, Campeche or Chanpoton; he wanted to avoid fighting before he reached Mexico. But he decided to stop at Tabasco, the frontier region of the Maya country, where Grijalva had found the population amenable. He had made plans how to explain his coming, not only at Tabasco, but wherever possible. He would say nothing about Velázquez or Cuba, but call himself an emissary of the King of Spain, who that year had been elected, as Charles V, Emperor of the Holy Roman Empire. He would say that Charles V, the greatest sovereign in the world, desired to extend his protection over American lands; and that his protection, besides material benefits, would bring a knowledge of the true God, and of His Son and Virgin Mother, a revelation of inestimable value. As we shall see, this line would enable him to throw off Velázquez's authority in a manner that was legal, at least on paper.

After anchoring outside the bar of the Tabasco river, he landed his troops at the Cape of Palms, about three miles from Tabasco city. This action roused the inhabitants. They swarmed on the river banks, armed to the teeth—archers, spearmen, slingers and men wielding two-handed swords with blades of obsidian.

Cortes arrives in Mexico

Surprised at so hostile a reception, Cortés sent Aguilar, the interpreter, to parley with some of the leaders. But they would not listen to requests for water and provisions. Cortés decided to force his way in. Next day took place his first battle, in which he showed his powers as a tactician. It had two phases. In the first he took by assault the city of Tabasco, which, as stated, was three miles up the river. This was effected by a frontal landing from boats, in which he had mounted his cannon, and a flank attack down a jungle path from the Cape of Palms, which he had reconnoitred in the night. Bernal says the Tabascoans had over 10,000 soldiers and they fought with ferocity. Nevertheless, Cortés established himself in the main square of the city.

The second phase was the more dramatic. Cortés learnt from prisoners that the Tabascoans had roused the neighbouring towns and were planning an attack in overwhelming numbers. They seem to have had a large standing army, probably for defence against the Mexicans, who were an aggressive imperialistic power. On hearing of this intended attack, he brought ten of his horses ashore. Next morning he sent his main force with his artillery out of Tabasco to meet the advancing legions, while he himself at the head of the troop of cavalry worked round to a hidden flank position. As the Tabascoans had never seen or heard of horses, he calculated that the surprise would be decisive. The foot and artillery met the Tabascoans on wide open ground. So numerous were they that the whole plain was covered with their forces. It seemed a waving field of plumes. Their faces painted in black and white bands, sounding their trumpets, whistling, drumming, 'they rushed on us like mad dogs', says Bernal. They did not notice that the Spanish cavalry was in their rear. Suddenly there was a sound of galloping as the horsemen charged. The apparition of ten unknown animals caused a panic. The Tabascoans not only had never seen horses; they had never seen or heard of beasts of burden of any kind. They thought the horses were supernatural creatures and, at

42

first, that horse and rider were one animal, a monstrous god bent on their destruction. They had stood up to the cannon, an equally novel weapon, though the smoke and flame had greatly alarmed them. But the horses were too much. They fled to the woods. It was the end of the battle.

On the day following, the Tabascoan lords came to negotiate peace. Among the presents they brought were twenty women, and among the women was one destined to take a leading part in the conquest of Mexico under the Spanish name of Doña Marina. She was the daughter of a Mexican noble. Her father died when she was a little girl, and her mother, after marrying again, wanted to be rid of her and gave her away. She was eventually adopted by a Tabascoan family. She is described as good looking, intelligent and not at all shy. Her value to Cortés was great at this moment, for she spoke both Mexican and Maya. As Aguilar spoke Maya and Spanish, she provided the means of communicating with the Mexicans. This was valuable enough, but her birth, cleverness and aplomb, and the distinction of her manner, made her far more than a mere interpreter. She became indispensable to Cortés in all delicate negotiations. Moreover, she grew very fond of him, and later on, bore him a son, Don Martin. She is referred to on occasion by Bernal under the name of Malinche. This is a corruption of the Mexican words *ce malinalli*, one grass of penance. In Mexico a person's name had an astrological significance; it indicated what would befall him. Marina's name, One Grass of Penance, was a name which a female born on a particular date would be given. The fortune of those born on that date would have a connection with dissension and war and the overthrow of old established things. That it was believed that Marina would be mixed up with troubles of this sort was probably the reason why her mother got rid of her. From the Mexican point of view she was an unlucky person, somebody dangerous to have to do with. From her point of view, however, strife would be advantageous, because she, being astrologically connected with it, would be in

43

her element and so would realize her inner potentialities. Since she was aware of the destiny foretold for her, she saw Cortés as the personification of the strife which would carry her to fortune. She had therefore a strong personal reason for faithfully supporting him. The more he was engaged against the Mexicans, the higher she would rise. In the greatest dangers she would be invulnerable. Later, when Cortés was identified with a deity fated to bring trouble, she as his attendant became semi-divine. His meeting with her was far stranger than he thought. On the threshold of mysterious Mexico she mysteriously had come to usher him in.

The Tabascoan lords were so humbled by the defeat of their thousands by a mere handful, so overawed by the horses and cannon, and now so charmed by the gracious reception they were given by Cortés, that when he called on them to acknowledge Charles V as their overlord, they made no objection. He had already symbolically taken possession of their land in the name of his sovereign by striking a tree with his sword in the presence of a notary, just as Balboa had taken royal possession of the whole Pacific by wading armed into its waters at Darien. At Cortés' seisin no mention was made of Velázquez, at which neglect his partisans had murmured protests.

Since the Tabascoans were now vassals of Charles, at least in name, it was necessary they should also become Christians. Cortés could not hope to instruct them, but he could give them a demonstration. Palm Sunday fell a day or two later. He asked them to make him an altar. On the Sunday morning he invited the nobles and their families to witness the Mass. First they watched the procession with palm branches, Cortés himself devoutly carrying one. Mass was performed in full canonicals by the three ecclesiastics who accompanied the expedition. The Tabascoans then saw Cortés and his captains reverently kiss the Cross. They were astonished and impressed, and, when shown an image of the Virgin with the infant Christ in her arms, declared 'that they liked the look of the great lady', as

Bernal puts it. Cortés embarked that night and before leaving got them to promise to keep the altar clean and put flowers before the Cross, for so would they enjoy good health and full harvests. That they believed the Virgin was a deity of some kind is probable. But they may have thought it prudent to placate their other deities by human sacrifice for the liberty they were taking of including her, even temporarily, in their pantheon.

The Spaniards had no time to inquire who the Tabascoans were nor, had they done so, were they qualified to form what we would now call a critical opinion. These people were not Mayas, though they spoke the language, but a distinct race which had been civilized far longer than the Mexicans. They were the inheritors, perhaps partly the descendants, of the Olmecs, who had created one of the classical cultures of Central America and had been especially noted for their colossal sculptures. At the time the Spaniards met them, the Tabascoans had come to be associated with the luxuries of life. They cultivated rubber, unheard of in Europe, but exported from Tabasco for use as paint, incense and medicine and for making the large balls used in the game called Tlachtli, like football because there was a goal, like racquets because played in a walled court, but like neither because the ball was propelled by movements of the hips. They were lovers of flowers, expert horticulturists who had been called in to stock the botanical gardens laid out on an island in the Mexico lake about forty years before the Spanish invasion, gardens which had no counterpart in Europe. They seem to have been able to remain independent despite Mexican aggression. The coast people whom Cortés was coming to next, the Totonacs, had lost their independence and were incorporated in the empire.

But though Cortés and his companions were not able to focus the Tabascoans in their cultural setting, they had sources of information which we do not possess. For instance, they had the twenty women on board. After Padre Fray Bartolomé de

Olmedo, one of the friars with the fleet, had baptized them, they were given as consorts to the captains, a sort of marriage that was recognized at the time. The women were all daughters of the Tabascoan nobility. On baptism, Spanish names were chosen for them with the noble prefix of Doña. Doña Marina was given by Cortés to the young nobleman Alonso Puertocarrero and did not become Cortés' consort until later, when Puertocarrero was sent as an emissary to Charles V. As it was possible to communicate with them through Aguilar, one may be sure that Cortés and his captains, during the four days of Holy Week that the fleet coasted along to its destination at San Juan de Ulúa, learnt from them many things about Tabascoan life that we should be glad to hear. The women were probably asked to tell all they knew about Mexico, its reputed riches in gold and its monarch, Montezuma.

Bernal describes how the veterans of the Córdoba expedition, such as himself and Pedro de Alvarado, began pointing out to Cortés, as they caught sight of them, the landmarks along the coast, the great snow-capped peak of Orizaba, a river to which Alvarado had given his name, and at last, a few miles short of San Juan de Ulúa, the River of the Banners where the Mexicans had waved to them. The weather was very fine, they were close in shore; the maize and cotton plantations looked well tended, the towns prosperous in their palm groves. Behind the tropic plain the mountains rose into the cool. As conquistadors, they had come to gain possession of this delightful land, to march beyond the mountains, see the marvels there, gather the gold, win a new empire for Charles, their king. The lines of an old song came into Puertocarrero's head, and going up to Cortés he quoted a verse, adding: 'That is what these gentlemen have been saying to you. You are looking on rich lands. May you know how to obtain the government of them.' To which Cortés replied, says Bernal: 'God give us the good fortune in fighting granted to Roland, the paladin. Then, with your Honour and the other gentlemen as leaders, I shall know well how to manage

46

it.' Cortés saw himself as an independent hero. That he was supposed to be under Velázquez's orders he no longer thought it necessary to pretend. Bernal ends the passage: 'At last our good fortune brought us to San Juan de Ulúa soon after midday on Holy Thursday, 1519.' Between this island and the mainland was a channel a mile or so wide, where the Spaniards could anchor the ships and be protected against the northerly gales. Their arrival was awaited. Montezuma was watching.

६5३

Montezuma

I have said that Montezuma was waiting, because he was expecting a god to come. So extraordinary a statement requires explanation. We have to ask who was Montezuma, who the Mexicans, what made them expect—like the Jews, for instance—that a god was coming, and why did they think Cortés was (or might be) that god.

As for the Mexicans, it is not too great a simplification to say that they were a tribe of Red Indians, who at some early unknown date left North America and in company with other tribes speaking the same language (called Nauatl, pleasant sound) slowly migrated south towards Central America, a sort of promised land to which many other tribes had preceded them. The original place of origin of all these tribes had been north-eastern Asia. In late Palaeolithic and Neolithic times wave after wave of hunting peoples crossed the Bering Strait into North America. For thousands of years they continued to move southwards, one behind the other. By the fifth century B.C. those who had reached Central America were already civilized agricultural communities. The early Central American cultures were in turn submerged by the hunters always pressing down from the north. But hunters on reaching Central America became civilized and developed their own culture. Seven principal cultures had risen before the Mexicans arrived in the thirteenth century. There had been the Olmecs, already mentioned, whose culture was co-terminous with that of the ancient Greeks. The Maya culture had been in existence since 300 B.C. There had been the Teotihuacan and the Toltec. Some still survived, others had disappeared, but had transmitted their ideas to their successors. The culture evolved by the Mexicans was the last, and incorporated many of the ideas they found in the country. They began to build Mexico city in 1324, scarcely two hundred years before the coming of the Spaniards. By 1400 they were the most powerful nation in all that region. They were a harder, fiercer race than any of their predecessors or present rivals. Their religion was more cruel and fanatic and their administration harsher. They were permanently organized for war and had subdued a great part of what is now central and southern Mexico. Their traders penetrated beyond their boundaries into Yucatán and as far as Costa Rica on the Pacific slope. A heavy tribute in kind was extracted from the regions they annexed, tribute which included clothes of all kinds, military uniforms, maize, gold, paper, chocolate, mats, honey, incense, jade, pottery, jewels, spears, feathers, cotton, rubber and tobacco pipes.

The Mexican court and nobility, a military caste, analogous to the Knights Templar since they were also ecclesiastical, were able to live in luxury, thanks to the influx of such goods, collected by tax-gatherers from no less than 371 subject towns, but they lacked many ordinary things enjoyed by their contemporaries in Europe. They had no cattle and so no beef or dairy produce. Having also no horses, they had no carts. They could have used hand-carts and barrows if the wheel had been in use, but it had only been developed for children's toys, though they seem to have used rollers to help them to move large blocks of building stone. It may be that they had magical reasons for not putting the wheel to practical use. The result of their not doing so was that all goods had to be carried by porters. Important people were carried in litters. Plenty of iron ore existed, but they had not smelted it and their weapons were made of wood pointed with stone and occasionally with bronze. To call them stone-age people, however, would be to employ a misleading label. They were advanced in many ways. They had a penal code and an independent judiciary. They were in process of developing the picture writing, which they had inherited from some earlier people, into an ideographic system like the Chinese. Their annals were recorded, they were astronomers and had an elaborate calendar. Their engineers were able to design causeways, bridges and aqueducts. Above all, their sculpture was of a very high order.

At the head of the government was a monarch who was elected by a Council of Six from among the members of his predecessor's family, the choice going to the man with the highest attainments. He was not called King, however, but First Speaker. The present monarch, Montezuma, was the second of that name. In its more correct transliteration from the Nauatl as Motecuçuma, it means the Courageous Lord. Montezuma was head of the army and the church, and governed through a Council of Three, consisting of the Commander-in-Chief who had the title of Snake Woman, the High Priest and the Governor of the City. He had succeeded in 1502 at the age of thirty-five and when the Spaniards landed was fifty-two and had been reigning seventeen years. Before coming to the throne, he was a celebrated man, and had been both a General in the army and High Priest. He is described in the Mexican chronicle included in the *Codex Mendoza* as 'learned, an astrologer, a philosopher, and skilled in all the arts'.

This account of Montezuma and his government, necessary if we are to estimate Cortés' problem, sounds so ordinary that it might apply to any country. But the government of Mexico had an extraordinary element in it, its chief element, the religion it fostered. Though there was a sovereign, a council, an army, a judiciary, a civil service, a treasury and tax collectors, and the duty of these officers was to direct policy, extend the

empire, dispense justice, maintain law and order, make grants
and pay expenses, they had another duty, an over-riding duty,
a duty to which all their normal labours were geared to con-
tribute, the duty of dissuading the supernatural powers from
destroying the country, or more, bringing the whole world to
destruction. In Mexican opinion, and in the opinion of all the
races which lived or had lived in Central America, mankind
was at the mercy of unseen powers which were not well-
disposed to him. These powers, when placated, dispensed
blessings. The sun rose, the wind swept the road for the rain-
clouds and the earth brought forth. If they were not placated,
their evil animosity would break out, and they took away the
blessings which they had vouchsafed. The very sun might
refuse to come back at the end of night. The Mexican government conceived that its first duty was to ward off the danger
of an angry heaven. It was not known why the gods were ill
disposed, though every effort was made to find out. That they
were certainly so was evident from the frequent earthquakes,
floods, thunderstorms and droughts. To soothe them they must
be given what they most coveted, not empty worship, not the
spectacle of righteous behaviour, not anything so easy as praise
or love, but the stimulating food they required to sustain them.
And that food was not the maize or fruit, the cocoa or fowl the
people lived on, but human blood and human hearts, torn
from the victim's breast and presented fresh, hot, still palpitating.

It is no exaggeration to say that the government of Mexico
was organized from top to bottom so as to be able to sustain,
and thereby mollify, the unseen powers with as many human
hearts as it was possible to give them. In the ancient past many
peoples have sacrificed human beings to gods. But though by
the sixteenth century the practice had long ago died out in the
civilized parts of the world, the Mexicans continued it, despite
the otherwise almost contemporary level of their civilization.
And they applied it with an atrocious thoroughness which no

people, either in Central America or elsewhere, had ever used.

The government could not expect its own people to offer themselves for immolation. Had it required them to do so, an economic crisis would have resulted, in view of the great number of hearts required. War was the only way to obtain hearts. For that reason the Mexicans were continually making war against the independent states on their borders. In such wars the main object of their generals was to avoid killing the other side. Tactics were directed solely to taking prisoners, and battles were broken off when enough had been secured. (This preoccupation with prisoners gave an advantage to a side that was not burdened with having to take them. Cortés was partly to owe his survival when outnumbered and his ultimate victory to this military error of his opponents.) So much was the taking of prisoners considered the greatest service a soldier could render his country, that he was automatically awarded promotion and decorations according to the number he had seized and brought in.

A paradox was the result. As the goodwill of heaven could only be retained by perpetual battle, peace became a dangerous state of affairs. A long peace, as it would mean little or no food for the gods, might lead to the total destruction of humanity. Only in war was there safety. It was a nightmare, but mankind had no choice.

One asks how the Mexicans arrived at so pessimistic a theory of the universe. An answer in part might be that a malevolent heaven had been a cardinal belief throughout the area from primitive times. In none of the cultures had a thinker arisen strong enough to modify it. Nevertheless, as will appear, there was a tradition that in former times a great teacher had declared that heaven did not require human sacrifice, though in the end his doctrine had failed to carry conviction. In short, the inhabitants of Central America had not advanced intellectually like those of the Mediterranean and elsewhere.

The propitiation of the gods by human sacrifice was not, as

the foregoing account might suggest, merely the simple butchery of captive victims. The most elaborate magical ritual had grown round sacrifice. The day and hour, for instance, when each god should receive his blood offerings, had been worked out in immense detail. The right time was determined by astronomy. The priests of Central America had not gone to the labour of calculating a calendar, as perfect or more perfect than any in Europe, simply for the convenience of knowing the dates. They had done so because they conceived it to be a matter of life and death to approach the gods at the most auspicious moments. The connection between the gods and the calendar lay in the belief that the gods (or some of them) were the heavenly bodies, the sun, moon, planets and stars. They pervaded other things as well, such as the wind and the rain, but their aspect as astronomical phenomena was very important. Sacrifices had to be synchronized with their positions in the sky. Not only did astronomy provide that knowledge, but in its form of astrology it could be used to find out the intentions of the gods and, if they were dangerous, to take precautions against them. A vast magical ritual was built up on this basis and supplemented the act of putting the victim to death. The religion had become such a tangle of rites and counter-rites that the Mexicans themselves had great difficulty in understanding it and knowing the right course to take in moments of crisis.

As this book goes on, there will be opportunities of illustrating how this system worked in practice. Suffice it to say here that Montezuma was surrounded by a corps of astrologers, augurs, necromancers and mediums; that he sought by many methods of divination—the interpretation of signs and symbols, the observation of portents, the calculation of numbers—to look into the future and to provide against occult threats. There was no end to the perils that threatened. Mankind might perish, not only because the gods turned on them, but also because the gods turned on each other. Science declared that celestial wars had occurred in the past and could happen again at ill-omened dates which were marked in the calendar. In result, the Mexican government and its priesthood lived under very great strain. Their theologians and scientists had reached terrifying conclusions and could think of no way of meeting the dangers they imagined except by feeding the unseen powers with increasing numbers of human hearts and using magic to deflect their malice.

Among the many deities were two of more importance than the rest. Tezcatlipoca (the Mirror that Smokes) was king of the gods, and associated with the night sky. He had another aspect when he was referred to as Uitzilopochtli (The Humming Bird of the Left). In this form he was the war god, a far more terrible god than the Roman Mars, and required hecatombs of victims if he were to continue to give victory. This premier god in his two forms was the especial guardian of the Mexican tribe. He had watched over it from the beginning and made it the great imperial power which it had become. Its prosperity and continuance were peculiarly linked with him. The second principal god was Quetzalcoatl (The Feathered Serpent). This was the god referred to above as the great teacher who had declared against human sacrifice. It was believed that in a remote past he had descended from heaven and taking mortal form had, as a priest-king, preached against the great tribal god. But Tezcatlipoca (Smoking Mirror) had succeeded in driving him out. He embarked on a magic raft on the coast near Tabasco and departed to an unknown region in the East. But before going he had uttered a prophecy: 'I will return in a One Reed year and re-establish my rule. It will be a time of great tribulation for the people.' This utterance was taken to mean that when he returned he would destroy the guardian god and punish the people for having abetted his expulsion. One Reed year occured at irregular intervals. The year 1363 had been a One Reed; so had the year 1467. Quetzalcoatl had not come on either of these years. The next One Reed year was 1519, the year we have now reached in this story.

Montezuma and his Council were not sure how Quetzalcoatl would return, but they surmised that, since he had gone east on his magic raft from a port on the Gulf of Mexico, he would come back in the same way and arrive in some curious craft from an easterly direction. Tradition was definite about his looks. He would have a white skin and a full black beard, a very unusual appearance for those parts. It would be terrifying to see him come gliding in. How ought they to receive him, what should they say? If he came, as his parting words implied, to take over the government, should Montezuma resign or should he resist, using magic or force? Yet to resist a god, one of the two greatest, a god to whom many temples were dedicated, and whose feast was a great celebration, would be very dangerous. It was a dilemma.

How angry with them was he? Hard to tell, though he could not justly accuse them of neglect, for though he had been driven away, he was still worshipped. True, they had favoured Tezcatlipoca's heavenly kingship. But Quetzalcoatl's feast was as grand as his. Cholula beyond the volcanoes was its scene and the merchants had the duty of making it as splendid as possible. In that town, not indeed the capital, but a rich city, the great platform of his temple rose up, its base sculptured with feathered snakes. It was the loftiest pyramid in the country, more than 250 feet high. His image stood above the altar. He wore a bird's mask, sign that he was wind god, a red beak surmounted by a crest, the face painted yellow, the tongue lolling out. On his neck was a jewel the shape of a butterfly, and he wore a feather mantle, red, white and black. Golden his socks and his sandals golden. Forty days before the festival the merchants bought a slave, the most beautiful youth they could find, and dressed him as Quetzalcoatl with butterfly jewel, feather mantle and a diadem on his head. Flowers were brought him and exquisite food. He went through the city, dancing and singing. For forty days he was the god and the people crowded to adore him. Nine days before the forty were ended, two old priests came bowing to him and said: 'There is an end to dancing and singing. Nine days hence you must die.' And if he were sad and danced without joy, they gave him a drink of chocolate and human blood, in which some drug—perhaps peyotl—was mixed, that rendered him insensible to sorrow, as if he were under an enchantment. For him to be sad, would have been to lessen the force of the magical ritual. The forty days ended, they took him at midnight and on the top platform before the image of Quetzalcoatl stretched him on the sacrificial stone, opened his breast and pulled out his heart. The heart was offered on a dish to the image which they spattered with his blood. The magic ritual had turned the victim's flesh into divine flesh, and that night it was eaten by the merchants, a sacred repast that gave them communion with Quetzalcoatl. At dawn they danced and sang the mystery: by killing Quetzalcoatl by proxy, they had given him new life. It was, as it were, a resurrection; he had died and risen from the dead.

If, then, this god, so much honoured, should return as he had sworn and demand the throne, would it be possible to refuse him? But was not Montezuma's first duty to the old guardian god of the tribe? It was a grievous predicament.

Moreover, a mystery lay inside the mystery. While on earth Quetzalcoatl had preached against human sacrifice, yet, in their worship of him they used this very sacrifice (though sparingly), and offered him the heart food which he had denounced. How explain that they conceived there were two aspects of his divinity, a dark as well as a bright?

Montezuma had little hope that Quetzalcoatl would not come on the next One Reed year (1519), for many portents had signified that tribulation was at hand. For a time the night sky was lit by a northern light; a volcanic disturbance caused the water in the Mexico lake to boil up and flood the city streets; the temple of the sun god went on fire; a spirit speaking in a woman's voice wailed at night: 'My children, my children, ruin is at hand.' Magicians were called in to interpret these signs.

They could not pretend that their meaning was good. Montezuma strangled them, for in magic it is some remedy to destroy the bearer of bad news.

Sign followed sign, a comet, an earthquake. Montezuma felt his nerve giving way. A calamity was certainly approaching. His sister, Papantzin, after lying in a coma for four days, a condition that was taken for death, revived in her grave and on being carried back to the palace declared that she had seen strange beings entering the country and bringing it to ruin. This profoundly shocked him, but not more than what he himself saw shortly afterwards. He was sitting on his mat of state in the building called the Dark House of the Cord, the monastic university inside the precincts of the great temple of the Humming Bird, as the war aspect of Smoking Mirror was called. 'The sun had inclined already towards evening, but it was still day,' says Sahagún, the Franciscan friar who a few years later took down the story from those, perhaps, who were present at the time. 'Some people who earned their living by catching waterbirds, got a bird of ash grey colour like a crane and brought it to show to Montezuma.' As he looked at it he seemed to fall into a trance, and saw on the bird's head a magic mirror in which was reflected an ill-omened constellation. This alarmed him and when he looked more closely into the mirror he was horrified 'to perceive reeds like men approaching, armed as for war and mounted on deer'. It seemed to him that he saw the landing of Quetzalcoatl.

Following this vision he sent orders that a watch for the god's arrival should be kept along the Gulf of Mexico. In May 1518 rumours reached him of the landing of strange men at Chanpoton and Tabasco. In June, Grijalva's fleet was sighted some time before it reached the River of the Banners. A messenger hurried to the capital to give the news. He came before Montezuma, and, according to the chronicler Tezozomoc, said: 'Lord and King, forgive my daring. As I walked on the seashore I saw a sort of hill moving in the sea, such as we watchers of the sea had never seen before.' Montezuma had the messenger killed and sent men down to the coast at once to check this report. They returned to say they had seen two towers moving about the sea. Investigators of higher rank were despatched and their report was a little clearer: 'We know not what people have arrived at the shore. We saw them fishing from a canoe and then going back to two big towers, on to which they climbed. Their flesh was whiter than ours and they had long beards and hair.' This report confirmed Montezuma's fears. Though exceedingly alarmed, he decided to get into closer touch with the bearded white beings and issued the orders that led to the banners being waved to Grijalva's ships. The visitors were to be received respectfully with fumigation and be given what they wanted. During Grijalva's stay of six days his men were carefully observed by Montezuma's emissaries, who forwarded to their master a description in the Mexican writing, a sort of hieroglyphic script which combined pictorial representation and ideographic signs. Before leaving, Grijalva was able, though without a Mexican interpreter, to make it understood that more Spaniards would be coming the next year.

After Montezuma had studied the picture script, which gave a more vivid impression of the strangers than could have perhaps an alphabetical script, there seemed to him little hope they could be other than Quetzalcoatl's forerunners. The next year was the sinister One Reed (1519), when, as they said themselves, they would be returning. We do not know the details of what was reported to Montezuma. Grijalva had no horses and he may not have had any cannon, but the report must surely have included a description of the size of the ships, so much greater and more elaborate than the largest Mexican canoe, of the armour, muskets, crossbows and steel swords, all such extraordinary novelties as hardly to be accounted for in the world of men. Unlike the Spaniards under Columbus who sailed west in the certain hope of discovering new lands, Montezuma, had he been able to sail eastwards, would have expected to find, not a new land, but the eastern paradise where Quetzalcoatl dwelt, just as the old Irish thought paradise lay westwards in the Atlantic. That the Spaniards had come from that paradise seemed to him the only reasonable explanation.

As he brooded over the complexities which loomed ahead, he wondered whether he could avoid his fate. Was there nowhere to flee to? Could he not escape and hide, for instance, in a cave? But in what cave could he, so great a lord, take refuge and it not be known? He consulted the Chief Priest and the inmates of the Dark House. There were adepts, they replied, who could show him how to reach the abodes in the Four Quarters, Mictlan in the North where the dead went, the Sun's golden house in the East, the realm of the Rain God in the South, and the palace of the Maize Goddess in the West. 'But,' writes Sahagún, who records this strange consultation between the monarch and his lords spiritual, 'Montezuma decided not to go, though the adepts promised to guide him. He resolved to wait for Quetzalcoatl. He took heart, he strengthened himself. Let come what might, he would brave it out.'

Yet his perturbation of mind remained acute. He practised austerities, drawing blood from the lobes of his ears with cactus thorns and throwing the drops against the images of the gods. With his own hands he sacrificed human victims at the altar of Quetzalcoatl, hoping that perhaps some word of assurance might come from the god through the tranced mediums in attendance. And he gave orders that dreams should be reported to him by the governors of his provinces. Those whose dreams were inauspicious he had put to death. Perhaps it was all a dream and thus he could destroy it. Sometimes he would direct that the beads, given by Grijalva and sent up to him, should be brought, and while he fingered them he would say: 'We are very astonished by the blue stones. See that they are well guarded. Should one of them jump away and escape, our lands, our pregnant women, would fall into grave peril.' In these and other devout ways he passed the time of waiting.

The watchers on the coast were ordered to redouble their vigilance. And sure enough in the year One Reed the dreaded visitants appeared. More extraordinary still, Cortés landed on the very day of that year when he was expected to land. According to magico-astrological calculations the indication was that Quetzalcoatl would land on his personal name day, a 9 Wind day. Cortés, having reached San Juan de Ulúa on Holy Thursday (April 21st) 1519, landed the next day, and that day was a 9 Wind day. His appearance (white complexion, black beard) was as anticipated. Moreover, he was wearing a hat resembling the hat which Quetzalcoatl was reputed to wear, and had on a black suit, since it was Good Friday, a further coincidence, for in the pictures in the magical books Quetzalcoatl's clothes were painted black.

❦ 6 ❧

The Landing of
Cortés-Quetzalcoatl

When Cortés anchored off the mainland on the eve of
Good Friday, the death anniversary of the incarnated
Second Member of the Christian Trinity, he had none of the
information contained in the last chapter, and no idea that he
was a god in mortal form whose second coming had been foretold for the morrow. At most, he may have surmised that, like
Grijalva's, his fleet had been sighted some days before, and
have hoped that the inhabitants, who greeted his predecessor
and consented to trade, would do the like with him. That he
was fulfilling a messianic prophecy and had already thrown the
country into a nervous convulsion, he would only learn as the
queer fact was gradually revealed by the behaviour of the Mexicans. When he did learn it, he would see it as a miracle which
prepared the way for his conquest, an ambition apparently so
difficult with his small resources that he can hitherto have had
little idea how to achieve it. As we shall see, he did not dare to
play the god, for he believed that the Mexican gods were real
devils. Besides, in his total ignorance of Mexican theology, it
would have been impossible. Nevertheless, so convinced was
Montezuma that he was the god that nothing Cortés said or did
would seem inconsistent with his supposed divinity.

The Landing of Cortés-Quetzalcoatl

'Within half an hour of anchoring,' says Bernal, 'two large canoes full of Mexicans came out to us. Seeing the big ship with the standards flying they understood it was there they must go to speak to the Captain; so they went direct to the flagship, and going on board, asked for the Tlatoani (Speaker).' Doña Marina came forward and pointed out Cortés. The Mexicans, after making the customary salutation by touching the ground with the forefinger and raising it to the mouth, said to him they had been sent by the local governor to inquire who he was, and supply him with anything he wanted. Cortés thanked them and offered wine, a drink unknown in Mexico and whose flavour pleased them. He also gave each of them glass beads. He had come, he said, to trade, and they need not feel uneasy.

The Mexicans then left to report to the governor. What they had seen was very exciting, though Cortés had said nothing to suggest he was Quetzalcoatl. Nevertheless the ship, weapons, armour, everything on board, were extraordinary. He was surely a divine personage, though his food did not appear to be hearts. But Quetzalcoatl ate but little heart food. He might well be that god.

On Good Friday Cortés disembarked his men, horses, dogs and cannon on the mainland, here a stretch of sand dunes, and pitched a camp. During the ensuing week or so a series of conversations took place between him and emissaries from Montezuma. It is difficult to give these in the exact order they occurred, but what follows is the gist of these curious meetings. Montezuma, it appears, had been informed of the Spaniards' approach about a fortnight before they reached San Juan de Ulúa. Though Mexico city was at least two hundred miles inland from the coast by the shortest route, news could reach it within twenty-four hours by runners organized in relays. By the time Cortés landed, the first emissaries from Montezuma had arrived on the coast. They had with them a man called Cuitlalpitoc (Big Bellied), a slave, and were instructed to sacrifice him should Cortés want to eat him or drink his blood. They also brought quantities of ordinary food, over some of which human blood had been sprinkled. Their instructions were to try and find out whether Cortés was really Quetzalcoatl or not.

These people came to the camp on Easter Sunday. The Spaniards had no idea that Cuitlalpitoc was an intended victim. He looked so grave and important (he had been fattened up for sacrifice) that they thought him an official. His gravity can be ascribed to his anxiety; he was anticipating a horrible death. Things however did not turn out that way. Cortés embraced his callers and in their presence celebrated the Easter Sunday Mass; it was chanted by Fray Bartolomé de Olmedo, who had a beautiful voice. Afterwards he invited them to dinner, during which he explained that he was sent by the Emperor Charles V to pay his respects to the great Montezuma in person, whose fame had reached the Emperor and with whom he wished to be friends. (At this time both Cortés and Montezuma were quite unknown to Charles.) As it appeared that Cortés did not want to eat Cuitlalpitoc, at any rate at the moment, the Mexicans now brought forward Montezuma's present of provisions. Sahagún records that on seeing that portion of the food which was sprinkled with human blood, the Spaniards felt sick; the blood smelled like sulphur. A feeling of diabolism in the air caused them to smell the fumes of hell. This blood food seems to have been a test. That Cortés refused it was additional proof of his identity with Quetzalcoatl. Montezuma had also sent gold jewellery, embroidered mantles and feather capes. Cortés had had the forethought to bring some articles besides beads suitable as return presents and now gave the emissaries for their ruler a carved arm-chair inlaid with lapis lazuli and a crimson cap with a golden medal engraved with a figure of St. George on horseback. Also, to impress them, he fired off his cannon and told Pedro de Alvarado to lead the troop of horsemen in a gallop along the strand. The Mexicans stared, amazed and intimidated, and ordered their secretaries to make careful notes in the picture writing. Before the party left, Cortés repeated that he wanted to come up to Mexico for an audience.

Sahagún has described the midnight scene in the royal palace when the emissaries arrived back to report to Montezuma. For a Franciscan, Sahagún had a scholarly interest in Mexican ritual that was astonishing for the period and he puts down his facts, however sinister, without adverse comment. Sometimes his descriptions make your hair stand on end, as in the present case. The emissaries, hurrying from the coast in long forced marches, arrived, he says, very late at the capital. So urgent, however, did they conceive their business to be, that they went straight to the palace and asked for audience at once. Though Montezuma had been waiting for their return with the utmost impatience, he had given up hope for that day and gone to sleep on his mat. But as he had left instructions to be woken if the men arrived, they were admitted, led down the long stone corridors and ushered into his bedroom. It was about 11 p.m. Advancing with lowered eyes, for no man was allowed to look directly at the First Speaker, they asked for permission to address him. But Montezuma, already informed, perhaps, by advance runner, that Quetzalcoatl indeed had arrived, would not allow them to speak in the informal setting of his bedroom on so grave a subject. A report, touching the descent of a god and having to do with a crisis the most dreadful in all Mexican history, could only be delivered with the proper ceremony. He gave orders that all should adjourn to one of the main halls. There were cages in the palace where captives were kept ready, so that at any moment of the day or night he could quickly offer them. As he deemed it right to open the proceedings with sacrifice, he now sent for several of these poor people, also directing that they be painted with some earthen colour, a detail of importance in the rite. After a short interval they were led into the hall. A private sacrificial stone stood there and on it, one by one, they were stretched, four priests holding fast the limbs and a fifth pressing back the throat with a collar. Then the sacrificer (perhaps on this occasion Montezuma himself)cut their hearts out and offered them to some aspect of deity, though to what is not clear. The blood was siphoned from the bodies and spurted over the emissaries. 'For they had been witnesses,' says Sahagún, 'of portentous events and had seen and spoken to a god and his companions.' Though no doubt the ceremony reflected the reverential care and dread with which the cult of divinity was practised in Mexico, one cannot help feeling that Montezuma was a monster and the sacrifice of the captives a ritual murder.

Anointed with the sacred blood, the emissaries were now purified to speak. Displaying their picture writing in support of their words, they began to tell of the wonderful things they had seen and heard. Of the cannon, writes Sahagún, they said: 'The sound of the command to fire them was very startling. The thunder following the command deafened us. The shot burst out of the cannon's belly with a spray of sparks. The smoke smelt horribly and made us giddy. When the ball hit a tree, the tree turned to dust.' Of the Spaniards themselves they said: 'They were armed in iron, with iron on their heads. When they mounted their deer, they were roof-high. Only their faces were visible, white and very lined. Some had black hair, some yellow, and the yellow haired had yellow beards. They did not eat human hearts. Their dogs were very big, with folded ears, great hanging chops, and fiery flaming eyes, pale yellow eyes and hollow belly. Tongues lolling out, they were always panting, and their hair was flecked like a jaguar's.' Sahagún adds: 'When Montezuma heard this tale, he trembled with fear and almost fainted.'

Montezuma was now fully convinced that Quetzalcoatl had landed, and on learning that the god wanted to come to Mexico city, he was overwhelmed with awe. As the upholder of the Mexican religion, he must welcome him and bow to his will, whatever it might be, even resigning to him the throne. As the head of the Mexican state, his duty was to his country. He could not surrender it to another. If, then, he must neither resist the god nor betray his people, a compromise must be found. Could he not persuade the god to return to his paradise? It might be done with gifts, perhaps, or by magic. Force on no account must he use. But if the god could be peacefully induced to change his mind and go, the crisis would pass.

Deciding to try this course, he planned to recognize Cortés as Quetzalcoatl by sending him the insignia of the god, as well as many other valuable presents. His envoys would also take a most respectful greeting, but would hint that a journey to Mexico city was out of the question. Along with them he would despatch the most adept of his enchanters who, by every means known to them, astrological and incantatory, would seek to deflect the god from paying him a personal visit.

The insignia of Quetzalcoatl consisted, among other things, of a mask worked in a mosaic of turquoise, attached to which was a lofty crown of long green feathers (quetzalli). The features of the mask were formed by the undulations of a snake. Besides the mask there were a mantle and a mitre. The envoys should dress Cortés in these things. They should also present him with a hundred loads of valuables. The most important of these were two circular calendars, each as large as a cartwheel, one of gold, the other of silver, elaborately engraved with astrological hieroglyphs. In addition, a quantity of golden ornaments were sent, some in the form of ducks and dogs, jaguars and monkeys, others being collars, necklaces and sceptres. Addressing the envoys formally before their departure, Montezuma is recorded by Sahagún as saying: 'Our Lord Quetzalcoatl has arrived. Go and receive him. Listen to what he says with great attention. These treasures that you are to present to him on my behalf are all priestly ornaments that belong to him.'

With the envoys went a party of what Sahagún calls 'sinister people, the enchanters, the man-owls, the witchmasters', who were instructed to ensorcel Cortés, entangle him in incantations

and cause him to go back. Among them was a man whose name
has come down to us in the Spanish form of Quintalbor. He
was the exact double of Cortés, whose portrait had been sent
up to Mexico along with the pictures of his guns, dogs and
horses. In Mexican magic the double of a god had various parts
to play. It is perhaps significant that this Quintalbor is reported by Bernal to have fallen ill later. His illness, if pur-
posely induced, may have been in the nature of a spell to make
Cortés ill and so persuade him to leave.

The envoys and magicians took the road for the coast in all
haste, a large party with their litters and porters, the important
among them in embroidered mantles, the porters naked except
for their loin-cloths.

Meanwhile Cortés and his men had remained in camp on the
sand dunes. It was exceedingly hot and the mosquitoes were
very troublesome. Cuitlalpitoc had been left behind to look
after the visitors. Happy that he had not been sacrificed, he
humbly tried to make them as comfortable as possible. He
procured plenty of food, including turkey, then unknown in
Europe, and covered their huts with palm leaves against the
sun. It took the envoys only a week to go and return. One
morning early they arrived with the presents. Cortés received
them with the affectionate embraces which were his charming
custom. The presents were laid out on mats and, when their
enormous value was perceived, the Spaniards did not conceal
their joy. But the message that came with them was not so
agreeable. Cortés was politely informed that to visit the capital
was impracticable, though there was no objection to his staying
on where he was for a while. The journey to Mexico city was
long and arduous, explained the envoys, food difficult to get, he
would tire himself out. Montezuma did not wish to put him to
such trouble. Cortés assured them it would be no trouble and
asked them to take back a message that if, after coming so far,
he failed to see Montezuma, the Emperor Charles, whose envoy
he was, would be very disappointed.

The Landing of Cortés-Quetzalcoatl

The envoys left, telling Cuitlalpitoc not to be so amiable. To feed the Spaniards up was to invite them to stay. To get them to leave was what was wanted. Supplies should be cut down. The enchanters were at work trying to force Cortés out. He, of course, was quite unaware of their magical attentions. But he understood by now that they all believed him to be some god, who, it had been foretold, was to come from the East. With Marina and Aguilar to translate and explain, he could not have failed to gather as much, but he made no attempt to take the role. Indeed he continued as before to represent himself as an envoy of Charles V and to invite them to see the Mass. Nor did he hide his detestation of their cruel religion. One is obliged to presume that he did not take seriously the mistake about his identity. It had been useful to him so far. He could not otherwise have landed without rousing the whole country to resist him; and there was the fortune in gold he had been given. But the misunderstanding might not remain useful. Without knowing what was in Montezuma's mind, one could make little sense of what had happened. The Mexicans called him a god, but asked him to leave. Well, he was not leaving. Somehow or other he would get to the capital. The fact was that he could not return to Cuba and Velázquez. He had to devise a way of going forward. So when, a week later, a second refusal to let him come up was received from Montezuma, he merely deferred the visit. 'Some day, please God, we will go and see him,' he told his soldiers.

€7]

Cortés Tricks Velázquez

Three months were to elapse before Cortés marched on Mexico. During this time (15th May to 15th August 1519), he made a political discovery which changed the military situation. The period also saw his transformation from the leader of an expedition sent by the Governor of Cuba, into the Captain-General of 'the very Great and Powerful, and very Catholic Prince, most Invincible Emperor, our Lord', as Cortés in his letters called Charles V. That Charles had never heard of him was no matter, as will shortly be shown.

Further back it was said that Velázquez sent some of his friends with the expedition to see that Cortés ran straight. These people, with the soldiers that they had brought, composed a substantial proportion of the force. Up to date Cortés had managed to deceive them. It will be remembered that before he left Cuba, Velázquez tried to arrest him. Nevertheless, Velázquez's friends stayed with the expedition. Cortés had convinced them that Velázquez was mistaken in suspecting him. Moreover, he handled them very cleverly, bribing and making them splendid promises. They wanted to go and believed they could guarantee that Velázquez would be well served. But now a trial of strength between the parties occurred. Cortés perceived that if he were to make his march on Mexico, he must be undisputed master.

Things came to a head in this way. Velázquez's friends

thought the time had come to return to Cuba. The expedition had been wonderfully lucky. For reasons not altogether clear to them, but evidently having to do with his religion, Montezuma had allowed the expedition to land and had made a present of a quantity of gold. But he had refused to see Cortés and plainly hinted, first by reducing supplies, and then by discontinuing them altogether, that he expected him to leave soon. There were large Mexican forces somewhere inland. The sensible course was to go now with the treasure and report to Velázquez. What else was there to do? They could not stay among the sand-hills indefinitely. To move to better ground and settle there would bring the Mexican army on top of them. As for marching on Mexico, the idea was lunacy. They had done very well; better go while the going was good.

Such were the arguments that Velázquez's friends put forward. But for Cortés to go back would have been as ruinous as it was risky to go forward. All the gold would have to be delivered to Velázquez, who, after deducting the Royal Fifth, would be entitled to dispose of the rest. He could not be relied on to share it out fairly. As Cortés was in his bad books, he might even have difficulty in getting back his expenses. Indeed, Velázquez might do worse; despite the big gold return, he might say—as was true—that Cortés had sailed against his orders and charge him with rebellion. In that case, Cortés would not only lose everything he had won on the expedition (both in reputation and wealth) but also be deported to Spain, thereby forfeiting his estates in Cuba. To return home ruined and penniless after fifteen years' work in the West Indies was a bleaker prospect than the worst risks that Mexico might bring.

How did he stand? If he could get rid of the opposition, he would have at his disposal a body of men, small but compact, resolute and daring, who would follow him anywhere. He was, by an almost miraculous chance, safely on Mexican soil. That Montezuma planned an attack was by no means certain; the cutting off of provisions proved nothing. (As we know, this estimate of Montezuma's intentions was correct.) His right, his only, course was to stay on, explore the neighbourhood, add to his information, and sooner or later a chance would present itself of marching on the capital.

The first step, however, must be to outmanœuvre the opposition and free himself from Velázquez's control. His experience as a man of law in Cuba suggested how this could be done. That one of the greatest *coups* of his life was achieved by a legal quibble shows that he had talents not usual among men of action. Besides being an able commander, he was a machiavellian schemer.

Under Spanish law it was permissible for a body of Spaniards, whether in Spain or in the Spanish dominions, to found a municipality and elect its officers if they obtained royal sanction. The officers of such a municipality were directly subordinate to the Crown and no one else could give them orders. Cortés now proposed to his supporters—the Alvarados, Sandoval, Puertocarrero, Escalante, and the rest—that the camp be called a town and the soldiers a municipal community. When the expeditionary force had thus ceased to exist, he would resign his command and offer himself for election to the council. They would then make him head of the judiciary and commander of the municipal forces. Charles V's sanction could not be obtained in advance, since they were too far away, but he would be informed at once by letter of the founding of his new town, which he would recognize if tactfully approached. Pending the arrival of royal sanction, legal fiction would allow that they were already holding from the Crown. Velázquez would cease to be their chief. His right to the gold would lapse and his partisans in the camp, if they raised objection, could be silenced.

Such was the plan which Cortés unfolded to his supporters. It could, he added, be carried through with all the correct formalities, as he had a public notary with him.

Alvarado and his other friends were delighted. To get the troops to agree, their natural loyalty to the Crown had to be exploited. They were told that, if they returned to Cuba, His Majesty would lose the kingdom of Mexico which Cortés planned to give him. As the soldiers believed Cortés could conquer Mexico, it was easy to make them think of Velázquez as a man whose lack of vision would deprive the Crown of a new domain. They also believed that if they returned to Cuba, the gold would not be shared out among them, but if they followed Cortés they would make their fortunes.

Two or three days sufficed to transform the army into a municipality whose elected head was Cortés. The camp looked exactly the same, the soldiers the same, but were not the same, as Velázquez's partisans soon found out. Surprised and indignant, they repudiated the transactions, but were immediately put in irons for contempt. The shock of this, the sight of documents and seals, of a pillory and a gallows, sobered them. Cortés was able to talk them over and their leader, Montejo, even accepted the office of chief magistrate of the municipality.

Charles V had now to be addressed. Accordingly, the municipal authorities of the Villa Rica de la Vera Cruz (the Rich Town of the True Cross), as the camp of huts was now called, wrote to the Emperor, acquainting him with the adventures of the expedition and telling how, for His Majesty's greater glory, they had founded a city in his new empire. They begged him to recognize what they had done and as a proof of their devotion sent him the whole treasure which Montezuma had given, though, as they pointed out, only the Royal Fifth was due. Cortés thought this sacrifice essential. It would be the weightiest argument in his favour. Velázquez had his agents at Court and they were ready to spend heavily. But Montezuma's gold was a bid nobody could beat. Though the poor soldiers got no more than they would have from Velázquez, they were talked into agreeing by promises of future loot. Cortés also sent Charles a letter, the first of a series. This first letter is not extant.

Cortés Tricks Velázquez

Captain Puertocarrero was entrusted with the duty of delivering the treasure and the letters. He set off for Spain in a fast ship.

It is interesting to know that some of the golden treasures sent home were much admired in Europe as works of art. Albrecht Dürer is recorded to have highly praised their craftsmanship. Some of the pieces later found their way to the British Museum. The mask of Quetzalcoatl, which can be seen there by the visitor of to-day, is thought to be one of them.

Having secured his legal position by this masterly comedy, Cortés now made the political discovery which changed the military situation and proved to be of the utmost importance for his plans.

The sand dunes opposite San Juan de Ulúa where the camp lay was in the country of the Totonacs, a people different from the Mexicans and whose culture, like the Tabascoans', was of much greater antiquity. They had built the great city of Tajín, famous for its richly decorated architecture. They were marvellously skilled carvers of stone, as all will agree who saw their sculpture in the Tate exhibition of 1953. The Mexicans had conquered them some years before. So far the Spaniards had met none of these people, their visitors having been exclusively Mexicans. But one day, after the final visit of Montezuma's envoys, Bernal and another soldier, who were stationed on the look-out among the sand dunes, saw five men coming along the beach. They approached smiling and asked by signs to be taken to the camp. Doña Marina and Aguilar were called to interpret, but reported that the men spoke a different language. However, two of them stated that they knew Nauatl (the Mexican language), and speaking in it declared that the lord of Cempoalan, a large Totonac town some twenty miles north-west, had sent them to inquire who the strangers were and to offer his services. Cortés gathered from their conversation that Montezuma had enemies. He was delighted to hear this and after flattering and rewarding the two messengers he asked them to tell their lord that he would soon pay him a visit.

Since the Totonacs were friendly, Cortés decided to move into their territory. He could get no more provisions where he was; the soldiers lived on the fish they caught. Accordingly one morning he struck camp and they marched along the coast, the ships keeping abreast, until they reached Cempoalan. Notabilities, carrying cones made of roses, met them at the gate and invited them to enter. Their lord was a very stout and heavy man, they explained, or he would have come out himself to welcome them. 'As we got among the houses and saw what a large town it was, larger than any we had yet seen, we were filled with admiration,' writes Bernal. 'It looked like a garden city, and the streets were so full of men and women who crowded to see us, that we gave thanks to God at having discovered such a country.' Soon they were in a large square of whitewashed houses. The fat lord was there waiting for them. Cortés embraced him. He was truly very fat. After polite exchanges, they were shown into a large apartment, where the lord left them to dine off turkey, cake and plums.

After dinner he reappeared, attended by his staff in rich mantles. Cortés again 'embraced him with a great show of caressing and flattery' and was given a present of gold, jewels and cloth. Said the lord: 'Please accept this in good part. If I had more, I would give it to you.' And he complained bitterly of Montezuma and his governors, saying that Cempoalan had only recently fallen under the Mexican yoke. All his golden jewels had been carried off and his people were grievously oppressed. There were thirty towns in the Totonac confederation, he said. Montezuma not only demanded a heavy tribute from them but also victims. Every year many of their boys and girls had to be sent up to Mexico for sacrifice. Resistance was impossible, as the Mexican forces were huge. More than once when the fat lord was speaking of his people's misfortunes he broke down and wept. (Bernal always calls him the fat lord because he could not remember his name.)

That some of Montezuma's subjects were disaffected was

very good news for Cortés. The Totonacs evidently sought his friendship in the hope of securing his help. The fact was that they had heard of the defeat of the Tabascoans by the Spanish. They now saw with their own eyes the horses and cannon. They knew of the Mexican embassies and that Cortés had been given the insignia of Quetzalcoatl. The prophecy that this god would return and be victorious was common knowledge. With him as an ally, their deliverance was certain.

Some days later an event occurred which threw a lurid light on the Totonacs' servitude. Their chief men were talking to Cortés when messengers arrived in haste to say that five Mexican tax collectors were about to enter the town. The lord and his counsellors turned pale. Some hurried off to receive the alarming visitors, others prepared them a room, decorated it with flowers, and started cooking a dinner. Presently five Mexicans arrived, attended by servants carrying fly-whisks. Their cloaks and loin-cloths were richly embroidered and their hair elegantly dressed. Each carried a walking-stick and a bunch of roses. They ignored Cortés and passed on their way, smelling their roses in an arrogant manner. After they had eaten their dinner and drunk their chocolate (an intoxicant as prepared in those parts) they severely lectured the Totonacs for entertaining the Spaniards, saying that Montezuma had forbidden them to be supplied. As a penalty, the Totonacs would have to provide at once twenty boys and girls for sacrifice.

The sequel illustrates the boldness and finesse which were characteristic of Cortés. He resolved to use the occasion to obtain a securer hold on the Totonacs. They should rebel straight away and so, for fear of Montezuma's reprisals, be obliged to fall in with his plans, instead of him having to fall in with theirs. And he would manœuvre their insurrection in so clever a way as to ingratiate himself with Montezuma. When therefore the fat lord consulted him on what to do, he urged him to arrest the tax collectors. 'I dare not do that,' he faltered. 'I will support you with my men,' replied Cortés. 'Your lordship is certainly a teotl (god),' he replied fervently. Though he still hesitated, he was soon persuaded to make the arrest.

The news spread rapidly to all the Totonac towns and threw the inhabitants into a fever of delight. They swore that they would pay no more taxes. The fat lord now declared he would sacrifice the tax collectors. (The Totonac religion was the same as the Mexicans', though human sacrifice was on a smaller scale.) That night Cortés arranged the escape of two of the Mexicans and had them brought secretly before him. 'You are at liberty,' he told them. 'Go back to Montezuma and tell him I saved you, and will do the same for your three companions.' Next day, he accused the fat lord of negligence and, taking the remaining tax collectors from him, transferred them to his ships.

The supposed escape of the two tax collectors terrified the Totonacs. Montezuma would immediately learn the full facts and send a punitive expedition against them. But Cortés reassured them. 'Anyone coming to molest you will be killed by us,' he told them with a confident smile.

From that moment the Totonacs were his humble and devoted servants. Montezuma, though very annoyed, decided not to punish them until after the Spaniards' departure. He still hoped that this would take place, though his enchanters had returned to report that Cortés was impervious to their art. We do not know what other measures he was taking. It may be assumed that he was sacrificing every day and consulting oracles. The answers he got may have encouraged him to think that Cortés would soon leave. At this time he sent down his two nephews to find out what was happening. They brought further valuable presents. Cortés delivered to them the remaining tax collectors, stating that he had rescued them out of friendship for Montezuma. And he sent him this message: 'I and my men are on our way to visit you.'

The words, when repeated by his nephews, were like the voice of destiny to the distracted monarch. If Cortés came on, irresistibly on as prophecy foretold, it would have to be borne. Yet, he himself would continue to try everything, short of violence, to avoid his fate. Of all the strange facts in this drama, the strangest of all is that he had it in his power to destroy Cortés and his five hundred men, but could never bring himself to give the order. His science compelled him to believe that Cortés was a divine incarnation. Prophecy, divination, portents, astrology, signs, auguries, the calendar, history —all pointed to the awful fact. Greatly learned and experienced in what pertained to deity, he was convinced that a god had come down, not to give a revelation and save him, but to take away his kingdom because of the wrong done by his ancestors, when this same god was driven from the country. To attack the god, to destroy him, would perhaps be to destroy the wind, one of his manifestations, the very breath of life, for without it the clouds would not come, there would be no rain, no vegetation, and all would perish. Therefore he would go on trying to placate this incarnate Quetzalcoatl, and thereby perhaps save his country. But if the worst happened, if the god could not be placated, if he himself must die and his people suffer great tribulations, these evils would be less than to risk convulsing the cosmos by putting an incarnate god to death. It must be borne in mind that the Mexicans were more terrified of the gods dying than of anything else.

When we turn from this haunted creature to Cortés, the Spaniard seems simple and robust. A bright adventurer of the Renaissance, without inhibitions or secret terrors, he wanted riches, glory and power within the frame of the Holy Roman Empire. Nevertheless, he also had his darkness. Both in his actions and what he symbolized he went beyond reason; in his actions because he had set out to do what reason could not sanction, the conquest of an empire with 500 men; in his symbolism because essentially he was what Montezuma thought him to be, not in fact an incarnate god, but a mortal through whom an immortal was to come in. Christ followed immediately behind him, or even led the way as he believed. That he was a vehicle of deity was both a darkness and the justification of any deed of darkness. So it is hard to say which of the two protagonists was the more mysterious, Montezuma awaiting the god, Cortés approaching with the Cross. Neither understood the other, yet in effect their thought was analogous.

8

Cortés Prepares

The time was now close for Cortés to march. He had so regulated his legal position that if he achieved a conquest it would be his, not Velázquez's. And he had made a conquest more possible; it had been impossible when he was not fully master. He had discovered, moreover, that not only were the Totonacs longing to throw off Montezuma's rule, but also other peoples between the sea and the capital. If he directed his march through their territory, the operation would become less hazardous. It remained, however, a desperate venture as far as his information went. With no reserve of arms and ammunition except what he carried, with no provisions beyond what the country might provide, and no hope of Spanish reinforcements to take the place of casualties, he was setting out in the face of an army hundreds of times larger than his own and armed nearly as well as the seven-eighths of it which had no horses, muskets or crossbows. True, he had represented himself as a peaceful envoy. But should Montezuma be angry at his impertinence in coming up without leave, the Mexicans might surround him somewhere in the depths of their country and, depriving him of food, rush his camp one dark night and overwhelm his exhausted troops. Even if some of Montezuma's subjects were disaffected, it was past reason to stake all on success. In general Cortés was not stupidly rash. On the contrary, he was prudent and cautious, took long views, was noted for his astuteness. His boldest actions were patiently calculated. How then account for his determination to do what no prudent general would do? It was no sudden decision; he had made it in Cuba. His men had long known of it and approved. He had even confided it to Charles V. The letter in which he did so is lost, but in his second letter to the Emperor he recalls the passage in the first: 'I remember that I offered to accomplish the impossible, for I vowed to your Royal Highness that I would have Montezuma prisoner, or dead, or subject to the Royal Crown of Your Majesty.' He could hardly have thought that as an envoy who had been refused audience he was inviolable. There seems but one answer to explain his certainty. Belief in their mission is characteristic of great men. Cortés believed he was fated to conquer Mexico. He could not have told why he believed himself chosen for the task. But he seems never to have doubted it. That was his strength. It was also his men's strength. Inspired by his confidence, they were as confident as he.

Before leaving on August 15th, he took an action likely to increase rather than diminish his difficulties. He deliberately cut his communications with home. His ships represented his only means of evacuating Mexico if he were defeated. He ran them ashore and totally wrecked them. He had, of course, his reasons. He did not see how he could control the ships after he had left. The sailors might sail them back to Cuba, where they would be very useful to Velázquez. There were a few malcontents, who might desert him and go on them. Once in Cuba these men would tell Velázquez what had happened and perhaps aid him in fitting out an expedition against the subordinate who had broken loose. There was a psychological reason also for the destruction of the ships: without means of retreat the soldiers would have to fight desperately. Moreover, the odd hundred sailors would amount to a useful reinforcement, particularly as about forty of his five hundred men had died of wounds received in the fighting at Tabasco. But none of these reasons, nor all of them together, would have justified a prudent commander in destroying his line of retreat. The ships could have been anchored with skeleton crews, their compasses and sails removed, the malcontents roughly treated and cowed. Only a commander with a mystical certainty of victory would have dared to do what Cortés did.

But another measure he took was of a precautionary nature. He made the region of Cempoalan into a base by building on a plain seven miles north of that town the Villa Rica de la Vera Cruz, which hitherto had had only a paper existence on the sand-hills opposite San Juan de Ulúa. The fat lord helped with labour and materials. Cortés set an example by carrying stones. Very soon the first Spanish town in Mexico began to take shape, with a market place, a church, an arsenal and a fort. It was arranged that Juan de Escalante should be left in charge of it. His garrison was to consist mostly of Spaniards too old or too ill to march.

The new town made the Totonacs feel more secure against Mexican attack. To cement their friendship with the Spaniards, the fat lord brought eight girls, daughters of the aristocracy, and wanted them married to the captains. Says Bernal: 'They were dressed in the rich embroidered costume of the country. Each had a gold collar round her neck, golden ear-rings and a maid.' One of them was the fat lord's own niece, and her he intended for Cortés. Unfortunately, she was very ugly, says Bernal. 'But Cortés received her and tried to look pleased.'

The offer of these girls gave Cortés his opportunity of talking to the Totonacs seriously about their religion. He said the captains could not accept the girls unless human sacrifice was given up. 'We had seen so many cruelties and infamies,' says Bernal. 'Every day we saw sacrificed three, four or five people, whose hearts were offered to the images of the gods, their blood plastered on the walls and their limbs cut off and eaten.'

This must stop, Cortés told them, if they wanted friendship and the protection of the Emperor.

The fat lord was much taken aback. The Totonacs' favourite deity was the maize goddess, though they also worshipped Smoking Mirror, the premier god. Maize was their staple food and the lord pointed out that to neglect the maize goddess would endanger the harvest. The other gods too were not to be trifled with. To abolish human sacrifice would be madness.

A stormy scene resulted. Cortés said that if they refused to throw their gods down from the high platform of their pyramid temple, he would do it. The fat lord, normally a most amiable fellow, flew into a violent rage and beckoned to his archers. Doña Marina, 'that excellent woman', as Bernal calls her, took it upon herself to say: 'If you shoot, we call the Mexicans in.' The threat was enough. 'Throw them down if you must,' said the fat lord resignedly. 'We don't consent, but we can't prevent you.'

Hardly were the words out of his mouth, says Bernal, 'before fifty of us soldiers clambered up the pyramid and threw over the images which came rolling down the steps, shattered to pieces. Some looked like fearful dragons as big as calves, others were half-men and half-dogs, hideous to look at. The lords and priests wept and covered their eyes. They prayed for pardon, saying it was not their fault.'

Frenzied by the sight, the archers seemed about to shoot. But Cortés caught hold of the fat lord. 'One arrow,' he cried, 'and I'll cut your throat.' His lordship was no martyr. He shouted at the archers to go home.

Calm being restored, Cortés addressed the crowd in his most engaging manner: 'From this on,' he said, 'I shall treat you as brothers. You can depend on getting all the help I can give you against Mexico. I have already warned Montezuma not to molest you or attempt to collect taxes. Soon we shall be marching to overthrow him. And since you have lost your gods and are sad, I will leave with you a great lady, who will be your intercessor.' And he explained to them who the Virgin Mary was. He would put her in the gods' shrine on top of the pyramid, but before she could live there, it would have to be cleaned.

This was done at once. The Totonacs, now quite pacified, scraped the blood off the shrine walls and the whole was white-washed. In the course of the next few days an altar was set up inside it, covered with a good cloth and decorated with roses. The image of the Virgin and the Cross were then placed on it. Extraordinary to relate, four Totonac priests consented to be made acolytes. They also had to be cleaned up. Bernal describes what they looked like before and after: 'They wore black cloaks like cassocks. Their hair was very long, covered with blood and so matted together that it could not be separated. They had cut to pieces their ears in sacrificing their own blood. They stank like sulphur and they had another bad smell like carrion.' After being washed, their hair was shorn and they were clothed in white cloaks.

When all was ready, Mass was celebrated on top of the pyramid. The altar was lit by wax candles made of local bees-wax, a novelty for the Totonacs who had never thought of using wax for lighting. The image of the Virgin was fumigated with the incense hitherto used for the gods. The most impor-tant lords from Cempoalan and the other towns of the con-federation attended. The eight girls were brought up and after admonishment were baptized as Christians. Their nuptials with eight selected captains received some kind of minor solemniza-tion. Cortés took the fat lord's ugly niece. About this time Doña Marina also became his consort, after Puertocarrero, to whom he gave her at Tabasco, had left for Spain with the dis-patches and the golden presents.

Bernal, the only eye-witness who has recorded this scene, treats it lightly; he was evidently amused by the fat lord, a cowardly, though somehow delightful character. But the reality was no farce. It was one of the occasions in Cortés' life when he gambled with fate, though in general he was not a gambler. By destroying the gods, he took the chance of destroying himself. His only way of getting to Mexico city was to keep in with the Totonacs. So far he had been very tactful with them. His men were punished severely if they stole the smallest thing. Then suddenly, with a reckless disregard for consequences, he outraged them to such a degree that they wanted to kill him. Bernal's explanation is that neither he nor any of his force could stand the human sacrifices a moment longer. So horror-struck were they that even the risk of losing everything seemed preferable to winking at the practice. The explanation rings true. One feels that in their place one would either have done the same or been ashamed of not having the courage to do so. Nevertheless, as in the case of the ships, the imprudence was great for a commander in Cortés' delicate position. But his luck held. He counted on that. It was as if he thought no one could stop him before his mission was done.

Bernal says that the Totonacs settled down quietly as the Spaniards' friends. 'From that time forward, they always showed us goodwill. They were especially pleased that Cortés received their daughters and that we took them with us when we marched away.' Had it not been that they believed Cortés to be the returning god, they could hardly have accepted his religion the way they did. That Quetzalcoatl would displace the other gods was part of the prophecy; his objection to human sacrifice was well known. On reflection, they must have conceded that for Cortés to roll down the images was the very thing to expect. The sight of the desecration had shocked them at the moment, but it afterwards made them the more sure that he was Quetzalcoatl. That he did not ask them to worship him but the Virgin Mary and the Cross was a mystery, as was his talk of a distant Emperor, whom they must acknowledge. But they were ready to leave it at that. On his departure they promised to look after the altar and keep the candles alight. Moreover, Juan de Escalante, Governor of Vera Cruz, would be given what help he required to finish building the town. They also sent forty of their best born and most intelligent captains along with the expedition to show the safest road to Mexico and introduce the peoples met with on the way.

9

Cortés Marches on Mexico

The march to the capital is marked on the map at this page. It entailed crossing two passes of about 10,000 feet and a desolate plateau of volcanic ash some forty miles wide. The total distance was over 250 miles. Besides the icy passes and uninhabited desert there were narrow valleys, stony ravines, rapid rivers, volcanoes. Moreover, the city of Mexico itself was one of the most remarkable fortresses then existing in the world. In the middle of a big lake at an elevation of 7,400 feet, it could only be entered along causeways, some of them over five miles in length. In short, Cortés had started on a march of immense danger and difficulty, whose military objective was deemed impregnable.

The departure was on 15th August 1519. In his Second Letter to the Emperor, Cortés says the expedition consisted of 300 men at arms and 15 horsemen, and explains that 150 men were left behind at Vera Cruz. When he sailed from Cuba he had 553 soldiers. If the figures are correct, he had lost one way and another about 100 men. The 100 sailors are not included in this calculation. A few of them went with Puertocarrero to Europe. But perhaps we should add 80 of them to the figure of 300. Call the infantry, therefore, about 400 men. We see, then, that his striking force was even smaller than we supposed. The

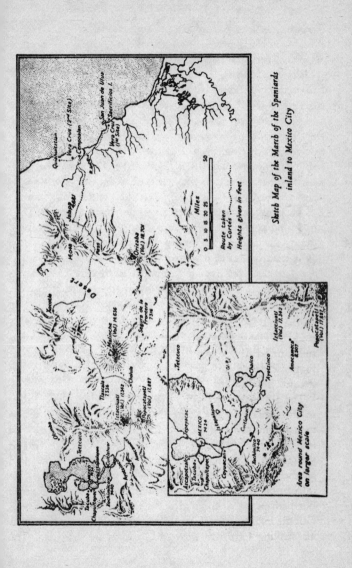

Sketch Map of the March of the Spaniards
inland to Mexico City

Miles
0 5 10 15 20 25   50

Route taken by Cortés
Heights given in Feet

Area round Mexico City on larger scale

Totonacs, besides contributing the 40 guides or aides mentioned, provided porters to carry the 14 cannon, the ammunition, and what essential luggage there might be. 'We poor soldiers,' says Bernal, 'had no need of help for at that time we had nothing to carry except our arms—lances, crossbows, muskets, shields and the like—with which we both marched and slept.' One should picture Cortés and his captains wearing steel armour, their horses also protected with some mail. The majority of the soldiers had cotton padded armour and steel helmets, and wore sandals of local make. Doña Marina and such of the other women who went—they did not all go—were obliged to walk. The three clergy were also on foot. One must add the dogs (greyhounds, lurchers, and perhaps mastiffs). The impression is of a resolute, brave, disciplined yet democratic, gang of adventurers. Such were the Conquistadors.

The road gradually mounted from the hot coastal belt to Jalapa at 4,681 feet, about fifty miles from Vera Cruz. This town was in the Totonac confederation and so the Spaniards were well received and fed there. On August 20th they were crossing the first pass. To the south, twenty-five miles away, reared up the giant volcano of Orizaba (18,700 feet) called, in Nauatl, Citlaltepetl (Hill of the Star). 'Hail fell and a wind driving down from the snowy mountains made us shiver with cold,' says Bernal, for they had no warm clothes. Descending from the pass they crossed the desert, a waste tableland, without inhabitants, marshy, sandy, ash covered and treeless. 'There was nothing to eat and the cold was intense.' By August 24th they reached Xocotla (Abundance of Fruit Trees), very hungry and very tired. Cortés explained his arrival by saying that he was an envoy on the way to the capital. Xocotla was one of Montezuma's tributary towns. The inhabitants had received no instructions about an embassy from him and were not too friendly. The Spaniards got a very poor supper and that was offered with ill grace. Afterwards one of the lords of the town began telling them what a wonderful and powerful prince was

Montezuma. 'He has a huge army,' he said. 'Mexico is a fortress of enormous strength. There are movable bridges at intervals along the lake causeways. If one of them is raised, it is impossible to enter the city. Moreover, the lake is full of fighting canoes, whose archers can attack a force on the causeway from both sides. The royal treasury contains gold of incalculable value.' This was alarming news, but Bernal adds: 'The more he told us about the great fortress and bridges, the more we wanted to try our luck against them, although it seemed a hopeless enterprise.' The remark is typical of Bernal. He thought no end of Cortés, but likes to remind the reader that his men were also wonderful fellows.

The Totonac aides had listened in silence to this recital of Montezuma's greatness, but now thought it time to impress on the inhabitants of Xocotla that Cortés was the bigger man. You don't seem to realize, they said, that you have a divine incarnation in Malintzin. (They had begun to call him by that name, derived from Malinalli (Marina's name) with tzin (lord) tacked on. Montezuma himself, they went on, has acknowledged him as divine, has invested him with the insignia of deity and also made him valuable presents. We notice that you have given him no presents; you have not even given him a good supper. It is not too late to make amends. And, frankly, we advise you to do so.

The Xocotlans were impressed and hastened to offer golden ornaments, collars, cotton mantles and women slaves. They asked about the horses: 'Are they dangerous?' 'Very,' said Cortés. 'And the dogs?' (There were only tiny hairless dogs in Mexico.) 'As bad as jaguars.' 'Have the cannon spirits in them?' 'Yes. We need only put the balls in. They do the rest.' After that they addressed him as a god. It seems that living in the depths of the country they had heard little of what had been passing on the sea coast. There is evidence, too, that Montezuma had bound his envoys to secrecy. He, of course, knew from the daily reports which his spies brought him that Cortés was approaching. The belief that he was Quetzalcoatl was yet further confirmed. The audacity of his advance and his insistence on a new religion were additional proofs of his divinity. But the Mexican religion was so complicated, that it was very difficult to be sure of the right measures to take.

The route that Cortés was following led from Xocotla through the territory of Tlaxcala (The Place of Much Bread). The Totonacs had told him that the Tlaxcalans were independent of Montezuma. They were the only Nauatl-speaking tribe that he had not reduced. He was continually attacking them, but had never taken their capital, which lay about half-way between Xocotla and Mexico. Afterwards he told Cortés that he could have taken it, if he had used his full force, but found it convenient only to take prisoners, to be used for feeding the Humming Bird on the Left. The Tlaxcalans, being his implacable enemies, were, said the Totonacs, certain to give the Spaniards assistance. As they had a large and experienced army, their help would be very valuable. Accordingly, after leaving Xocotla, a sinister place, where human sacrifice was so common that Bernal insists that he counted no less than 100,000 skulls of victims, Cortés sent Totonac envoys ahead to Tlaxcala to suggest an alliance, 'with a letter, though we knew they could not read it and, as a present, a red fluffy Flemish hat'. (Spanish head-gear had already intrigued the Mexicans because some of it was thought to resemble the ritual hats worn by the gods.)

Like the Xocotlans, the Tlaxcalans were not fully informed about what had taken place by the sea. The story told them by the envoys from Cortés that divine beings were coming towards them, accompanied by Totonacs, subjects of Montezuma, and supported apparently also by some Xocotlans, sounded to them like a Mexican ruse. Montezuma himself had perhaps arranged it, thinking that way to overpower them by guile. The state was a confederacy, ruled by a Council of Four, representing four principal towns. These four now resolved to resist Cortés with their army of 60,000 men. The envoys failed to dissipate their suspicions and contrary to diplomatic usage were put in a cage with other victims for sacrifice.

When his envoys did not return, Cortés, who had halted to wait for them, continued on his way to Tlaxcala, assured by the Totonacs that all would be well. After a while he met the envoys on the road. They had escaped from their cage and now told him the news in terrified voices.

It was certainly very bad news and gave matter for serious thought. But there was nothing to do but go on. The Spaniards were now irretrievably launched on the adventure. Cortés had beaten the Tabascoans in battle and had imposed his will on the angry Totonacs. But these were Gulf peoples, less hardy and warlike than the highlanders of Tlaxcala, who, thanks to Montezuma's annual raids, were permanently on a war footing. Elsewhere it has been said that the Spaniards, except for their horsemen, crossbowmen, musketeers, and park of guns, were armed with weapons similar to their adversaries'. True, their steel swords were handier than wood and obsidian swords and could be used for thrusting while the Tlaxcalans' were good only for hacking. They also had steel helmets. But the Tlaxcalans used a quantity of missile weapons, slings, bows and a spear propelled by a thrower, a mechanical device which added range and accuracy. With their enormous preponderance of numbers they were formidable adversaries. Cortés and his men, however, had advantages of a less tangible kind, though whether these would compensate for their great numerical weakness could not be foreseen. Their horses, cannon, etc., were novelties and worth far more than the number of them seemed to warrant. In military tactics, as was to be disclosed, they were superior; and they had greater skill with their arms. As a body they were more coherent, more educated as individuals, more methodical in their discipline. And they followed one man, who apparently could not be frightened, could not even imagine defeat, and who, though always in the thick of the fight, remained cool and collected. Cortés was the Spaniards' great advantage. Bernal, though not a panegyrist, compares him to Julius Caesar. Certainly he stands as one of the greatest of commanders in the field. There was nobody on the Mexican side to compare with him. His reputed divinity was a further asset. Though the Tlaxcalans were not ready to admit that he was Quetzalcoatl, they did not go so far as to deny that he might be. To find out his identity, they would attack. If he was the god, it would soon become clear, for they would be unable to overcome him. In that case, they would get him to forgive them their resistance by inventing some plausible excuse, such as blaming unruly levies. If he was not the god, then he would be captured, sacrificed and eaten.

It was by now August 31st. The Spaniards had been on the march for a fortnight. While they were ascending a valley, twenty-five miles from Tlaxcala, they came to a stone wall which spanned it from one side to the other. In the centre was a curious gate which had this form—

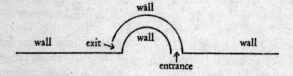

On each of the semi-circular walls was a parapet. Whoever entered the narrow passage of the gate could be attacked from above on both sides. But the whole was unguarded. Looking at it the Spaniards wondered whether this was a trick to get them into what might be impossible to get out of. However, they passed through the gate and continued the advance. Their guides said that they were now inside Tlaxcalan territory. The frontier had not been defended because it was the cardinal principle of Central American strategy to entice an enemy in and then capture him for sacrifice to the gods. The Spaniards, of course, did not know this.

They had not gone far before they came on some Tlaxcalan

scouts. Horsemen were ordered to gallop ahead and take a prisoner for interrogatio 1. The scouts resisted. Suddenly 3,000 Tlaxcalan soldiers sprang an ambush. The Spanish main body hurried up and used their fire-arms. The Tlaxcalans fought stubbornly but were gradually driven off, leaving seventeen dead and many wounded. The Spaniards had four wounded, one fatally.

Night fell and a camp was pitched. Nearby many farm-houses were visible amid fields of maize. But the inhabitants had fled and taken their stores of food with them, including their dogs, the small hairless kind which were bred for the pot. These foolishly returned later to the farm-houses and the Spaniards ate them. No attack was made during the night.

Next morning Cortés continued the advance. To the infantry the orders were—keep your ranks at all costs. To the cavalry—charge in parties of three, aim at the face, don't go far and return at once.

Presently they sighted the advance body of the Tlaxcalan army, a force of 6,000 men. The officers were in plumed or animal head-dresses, with banners attached to their backs. Their uniforms had devices denoting rank and decorations for valour. Their men were ranged in battalions, but massed rather than in lines. Drums, trumpets and whistles announced an attack. Cortés quickly sent three prisoners to parley and repeat that he was an envoy with no hostile intentions. But it was useless. With loud shouts the Tlaxcalans made at them. The Spaniards had formed a square covering the baggage, with the cannon on the wings and the horsemen in front. When it came to close quarters, the Tlaxcalans were hampered by their custom of having to take as many prisoners as possible for sacrifice. It was not easy to pinion a Spanish swordsman. In trying to do so you exposed yourself to his thrust. Even so, it was a desperate mêlée, particularly as the ground was too broken for the cavalry to charge, and not open enough for the cannon to be used to full advantage. By careful manœuvring, says Bernal, the Spaniards managed to reath a level stretch where the horse and artillery had a better chance. 'But as the battle went on, the enemy surrounded us on all sides, so that we could do little or nothing. Our lives were in great danger, for they were so numerous that they could have blinded us with handfuls of earth.' At this moment one of the precious horses was killed. 'They cut her head off with a two-handed broadsword so that it hung by the skin.' The Tlaxcalans were elated at this success, for they were not sure that the horses could be killed. Bernal heard afterwards that they offered the horseshoes along with the Flemish hat to the gods.

The Spanish column, however, remained unbroken and presently the Tlaxcalans, who had lost several high officers, disengaged and fell back in good order on their main army. The Spaniards entered a nearby group of pyramid temples, which made a convenient fortress. Their total casualties were surprisingly light, only fourteen wounded and one killed. After a dinner of turkey and little dogs, found in the neighbouring houses, they were able to get some sleep, for again there was no night attack. It was contrary to the military conventions of the country to fight after dark.

But the situation looked very black. It was learned next day that the main Tlaxcalan army numbered 50,000 men. As the Spaniards had barely escaped in a battle with 6,000, it seemed that their doom was sealed. 'As we were but human and feared death, many of us, indeed the majority, confessed to the Padre de la Merced and to the priest, Juan Díaz, who were occupied all night hearing us repent of our sins,' wrote Bernal.

Cortés always believed in the offensive. Instead of waiting in his temple fortress to be attacked, he sallied out a day or two later and met the Tlaxcalan army in the open. Bernal describes the scene in these words: 'All the plain was swarming with warriors and we stood four hundred men in the midst. We knew for certain that this time our foe came with the determination to leave none of us alive excepting those who would be sacrificed.'

Again Cortés' luck held. Had the Tlaxcalans been well led, nothing could have saved him. But it seems there was division in their command. The Council of Four who controlled the confederacy was no longer of one mind. Their failure with an ambush of 3,000, and an onslaught by 6,000, against a force of 400, led two of the Four to conclude that Cortés must be the god he was alleged to be. In that case he could not be defeated. Moreover, as the god, he could not be in alliance with Montezuma, as the prophecy was that the god would make an end of Mexico. He had offered them friendship. They would do well to accept it. The consequence was that the whole 60,000 did not make a concerted attack. Some part of them, perhaps half or more, held off. Nevertheless, the remainder strove to overwhelm the Spaniards. But they do not seem to have known how to break their formation. The Spanish foot stood firm, firing and thrusting. The riders made short dashes and managed to avoid being pulled off their horses. There were critical moments. Of one of them, Bernal says: 'I saw our troops in confusion. The shouts of Cortés and the other captains failed to make them close their ranks. So many of the enemy charged down on us, that it was only by a miracle of sword-play that we made them give way and so were able to re-form.' At last the Tlaxcalans seemed to lose heart; and after one of their chief captains had been killed, they disengaged. In his Second Letter to the Emperor Cortés says: 'In spite of being surrounded by such a multitude of people, brave and skilled in fighting, and with so many missile weapons, we came out little damaged except for the labour and fatigue of fighting and our hunger. It truly appeared that God battled for us.'

Cortés attributed his success to divine help, the Tlaxcalans explained it as due to Cortés' own divinity. Those who believed this before the battle were confirmed in their belief. Others, till then unconvinced, began to believe it. Magico-astrological tactics had been used. Cortés had been attacked from the four quarters. That in none of the four quarters was he vulnerable, proved that his power was of a supernatural order. There are allusions in the original authorities to other magical attempts to stop him and test his powers. Threads with papers strung on them bearing occult diagrams are mentioned as having been stretched across his path. That he was immune to such spells followed if he was divine. Thus, it was unnecessary for him to play the part of the god. His being unafraid of magic and impervious to it was a more convincing proof of his identity than anything he could have devised.

There followed a week or so of attacks on the temple fortress by the section still sceptical of Cortés' divinity, and of attempts to negotiate with him by the rest. He was able, however, to slip out at night and raid the neighbouring villages, inflicting heavy casualties when resisted, and carrying away provisions. But every time he lost a few more men killed and had several wounded. Though undefeated, he was being worn down. His days were numbered, if the Tlaxcalans kept it up.

His troops began to show signs of nervous strain. What was happening behind the scenes in Tlaxcala? It was impossible to be sure. Writing of this trying time to the Emperor, Cortés says: 'There was no one amongst us who was not frightened at having penetrated such a distance into this thickly populated country. We were so entirely without hope of help from anywhere.' A section of his men wanted to retreat. The right course, they said, was to fall back on Vera Cruz, get reinforcements from Cuba and advance again later. 'I was listening where they could not see me,' writes Cortés, 'and I overheard them say that if I had gone mad and wanted to advance still further, until I was where it was impossible to withdraw, they need not do the same. They would return to the coast. If I went with them, well and good. If not, they would go without me.' Bernal, brave though he was, confesses that he too felt very bad. 'One morning when we awoke and saw how many of us were wounded, some even with two or three wounds, how weary we were, how many were sick and in rags, and how already forty-five had died in battle or from disease or chills, and the Captain himself was suffering from fever, we began to wonder what it was all leading to. How could we march on the capital and face the great army of Montezuma when the soldiery of a country town like Tlaxcala had been able to reduce us to such straits?'

The only one, he goes on, who remained calm and confident was Doña Marina. 'She heard the Tlaxcalans shouting they would kill and eat us. She had seen us surrounded in the battles. She knew how wounded and sick we were. But never once did I notice the slightest sign of fear in her face. She had a courage, the like of which no woman has ever had.' Her courage was fortified by her horoscope. The more battles there were, the more she would prosper. In the Tlaxcalan pictures of her we possess she is shown carrying a shield in battle.

Having overheard their fears, Cortés gave his men a heart-to-heart talk. He began by praising their extraordinary hardihood. There was not another company of Spaniards in the wide world who would have fought with such courage. 'If you had not shown such valour,' he said, 'we should have perished. When I remember seeing us surrounded by so many companies of the enemy and watching the play of their broadswords so close to us, it even now terrifies me, especially when they killed the mare with a single sword cut. Had you faltered, we should have been lost.' But they had not faltered. They must not falter now. 'We are in a position to win the greatest kingdoms and dominions in the world.' And he appealed to their loyalty to Charles V and to the Church of Rome. The Emperor would receive a new empire, greater than what he already possessed. The Church would be able to evangelize a greater number than ever before in its history.

Both these arguments had great weight with his hearers. They had come on the adventure primarily to make their fortunes. But they also wanted glory, glory as the Emperor's paladins, glory as the Church's crusaders.

Cortés kept his strongest argument for the last, the argument of self-preservation. 'Gentlemen,' said he, 'it is clearly no good to go back a single step. If these Tlaxcalans were to see us retreat, the very stones would rise up against us. We should lose our reputation as gods and seem no better than cowards. Even our friends the Totonacs at Vera Cruz would turn on us. So, if one way is bad, the other is worse'. Writing to the Emperor, he reported: 'They recovered their spirits and I won them to my purpose, to do as I wished, which was to complete the undertaking I had begun.'

Cortés divined correctly that the bolder his front the more the Tlaxcalans would be convinced of his divinity, though it was not boldness as such that impressed them, but boldness springing from superior magical resources. And now at last, on September 20th, after he had been in his improvised fort for about seventeen days, supplied with provisions by one section, and attacked by the other, a deputation arrived with offers of peace and a cordial invitation to stay at Tlaxcala. It was headed by the Commander-in-Chief, clad in a splendid red and white cloak. After a respectful obeisance, he ordered incense to be burnt. Cortés in his most cordial manner seated him by his side. 'I represent the united Council of Tlaxcala,' said the General. 'We want to be excused for our attacks. The fact is that we did not know who you were. Montezuma is a crafty fellow. We were convinced he was using you to gain an entrance here and take what no Mexican has ever been able to take.' The General was tall, broad shouldered and well made. His face was long, his complexion coarse. He was about thirty-five and held himself with dignity.

Cortés pointed out that his envoys had made it clear who he was. The General replied that the misunderstanding was now over. The entire population of Tlaxcala was anxiously awaiting his arrival and would give his troops a rousing welcome. The confederacy wanted an alliance. They were ready to acknowledge the overlordship of the Emperor.

Who this vague distant personage was, they can have had no idea. If Cortés was Quetzalcoatl, the Emperor would have to be the supreme deity. In the mythology of the country, the gods, including Tezcatlipoca, the king of the gods, were subordinate to a yet higher power called Ome Teuctli (The Two), as if heaven were a confederacy with a Council of Two. In the magical book, now called the *Codex Vindobonensis*, there is a picture of The Two investing Quetzalcoatl with the insignia of the mask, the shell trumpet, the feather-fringed skirt and a hat, which was thought to resemble the high hat which Cortés wore when he first landed. The same picture shows Quetzalcoatl descending to earth from heaven by a rope ladder, not unlike the one used by Jacob. The picture, certainly known to the Tlaxcalan leaders in one of its forms, may well have been in their minds when Cortés talked of Charles V through the distorting medium of, first, Aguilar and then Doña Marina.

Cortés accepted the invitation to move to Tlaxcala, distant ten miles along the road to Mexico.

At about this time envoys also arrived from Montezuma. He had been watching with anguish the advance of the Spaniards. When he heard that the Tlaxcalans had mobilized to resist them, he hoped they would turn back. If I have interpreted correctly the religious belief that governed his policy, he dared not wish them to come to bodily harm, but if they themselves decided to go home, then his dearest wishes would be realized. When news reached him that Cortés was not withdrawing, the envoys were despatched to find out what exactly he was doing and to give him a further lavish present, which might perhaps turn the scale and induce him to go. 'He sent word,' wrote Cortés to Charles, 'that I should say how much I wanted to give Your Highness as an annual tribute of gold, silver, precious stones, slaves, cotton, mantles and whatever else might be acceptable. He would give all that was asked, if only I would not visit him in his city.' Montezuma was enormously rich because he and his predecessors had piled up in the palace a vast treasure from the tribute exacted from the subject towns. The quotation, however, should not be taken to mean that Montezuma agreed to become Charles's vassal. That was only the way Cortés put it. What he actually did was to offer Cortés himself any sum he liked to name, if he would go away.

Cortés thanked the envoys for the present and the offer, but said he would postpone his answer until he had settled his affairs with the Tlaxcalans. The Mexican envoys remained in his camp awaiting his pleasure, and were present when he received the Tlaxcalan General. The submission of Tlaxcala, says Bernal, was a heavy blow to them, 'for they fully understood that it boded them no good'. A Tlaxcalan alliance meant that Cortés would not go back.

News of it was sent to Montezuma. Sahagún has a picture of the consternation that prevailed among the inhabitants of the capital. There was no longer any secret about Cortés' approach, his identification with the god, and the revolution which he intended to inaugurate. At Tlaxcala he was only sixty miles away or, by the main road through Cholula, eighty miles. 'Montezuma despaired,' writes Sahagún, 'and the people were much alarmed at what might happen in the city. They gathered in knots to discuss the news. They hurried hither and thither, let their heads hang low and greeted each other with tears in their eyes. They caressed the heads of their small children, murmuring: "How will you bear the horrors that are coming upon us?"'

One must not forget that all the Mexican gods were vengeful cruel beings, and that though Quetzalcoatl was a milder god, as shown during his previous incarnation, he also had his darker side and one of his titles was Lord of the Twilight. If our scientists one day were to tell us that a comet was advancing to consume us, we could not dispute their reading of the heavens. So the Mexicans, assured by Montezuma, who as head of the priesthood was the greatest living expert on magical science, a subject as difficult to understand as our mathematics, that a catastrophe was approaching, could only accept as true what he told them.

It is interesting to reflect that Cortés, in the world of appearances, corresponded closely with the anticipations of magical science. He also had a bright and a dark side. He was the agent of an enlightenment, the harbinger of a vast field of new ideas. But he was also bringing death and destruction

ξ10β

Cortés at Tlaxcala

A few days later Cortés marched to Tlaxcala. The Totonac city of Cempoalan had been surprisingly beautiful, but Tlaxcala surprised him yet more. 'It is so large and admirable,' he told the Emperor, 'that although I will omit much that I might say, the little that I shall say is almost incredible. It is far larger than Granada and very much stronger. Its population is many more and its provision better. A huge market, jewellers' shops, as good crockery as anywhere in Spain, barbers and chemist shops and public baths. Order and politeness everywhere in the streets; the people as intelligent as the Moslems. As far as I can judge, the government resembles that of Pisa or Venice.'

Into this large city, so confusingly like a European city, but not really so, the Spaniards entered on September 23rd. The populace welcomed them, as divine beings should be welcomed. An incarnated divinity looks like a man. But these people were not deceived by the mortal appearance of the Conquistadors, for they now knew for sure that they were gods. Besides the crowd of leading men waiting to receive them outside the walls, numerous priests came forward and fumigated them with copal incense burning in pottery braziers. The ears of the priests were bleeding because that day they had offered their blood to the gods, to placate them, one supposes, on so momentous an occasion. 'They lowered their heads as a sign of humility when they saw us,' writes Bernal. The streets and the flat roofs of the houses were full of people, all with happy faces. Men and women pressed up to give roses. Quarters had been prepared for the visitors in a building opening off a large courtyard. Each soldier found a mat bed and blankets. 'We were astonished at the courtesy and affection they showed us. During the twenty days we stayed, there was always more than enough to eat.'

The senior member of the Council of Four was blind. He asked to be led up to Cortés and felt him over his head, face and beard, and over all his body. And he said: 'Malintzin, I have a beautiful unmarried daughter and I would like to give her to you.' As Cortés had already two consorts, Doña Marina and the ugly niece of the fat lord of Cempoalan, though the latter had been left behind, he gave the girl to Pedro de Alvarado, saying he was his brother. When she was baptized, which took place shortly afterwards, she was christened Doña Luisa. Bernal says that she had a daughter by Alvarado who married a cousin of the Duke of Albuquerque. The Tlaxcalans were, like the Mexicans, one of the Red Indian tribes of North America, who had migrated to Central America some two or three centuries earlier. That their daughters were now able to move in the best Spanish society shows the level of civilized manners to which the tribe had attained. The episode is illuminating in other ways. The Spaniards had no colour bar. A lady, provided she was baptized, was treated as a lady; the shade of her complexion was of no consequence.

Cortés, with his loathing of human sacrifice, at first wanted to force the Tlaxcalans, as he had the Totonacs, to get rid of their bloodthirsty deities. His companions, however, protested that this would be the height of imprudence. Rolling the images down at Cempoalan had been a close thing; here it would be plain suicide. 'It would be better, your Honour,' said the Padre de la Merced, 'to lead these people gradually to perceive the superiority of our religion.' The project was dropped. But Cortés got permission to put an image of the Virgin and a cross in a new pyramid temple close by. That was where, after Mass, Doña Luisa was baptized and with her some other girls who had been offered to the Captains.

Cortés now turned his attention to finding out all he could about the Mexicans. The Council of Four told him that Montezuma could put 150,000 men into the field. Some of his soldiers, however, were conscripts from subject cities, who did not fight hard and who used to give warning of a raid. The Four showed battle pictures painted on cloth, which illustrated in detail how the Mexicans fought. They also described exactly the layout of the capital, the depth of its lake, the width of the causeways, the number of bridges, the canals, the water supply and the principal fortifications.

Cortés had now to decide on his next step. He was going to the capital, but how and when? His alliance with the Tlaxcalans had completely changed his situation. They were an independent military power right in the middle of the Mexican dominion. If they marched with him, his chance of victory would be greatly increased. They appeared to be anxious to go with him.

The situation, however, was complicated. Cortés did not know that Montezuma, for magical reasons, had resolved never to use his troops. All he knew was that Montezuma had not attacked him so far. His fictional envoyship had perhaps protected him. No Mexican army had stood across the way, when the Spaniards were toiling up from the coast. Though there was a small permanent Mexican garrison in Xocotla, it had made no sign; nor had it been reinforced. But was that really the explanation? He had come against orders and his suite was not like an ambassador's. Perhaps Montezuma was afraid of him? If so, why? The Tlaxcalans had not been afraid to fight him. Or was it guile? Was Montezuma luring him on, so as to overwhelm him the easier? But that did not make sense either. By allowing him to come on, Montezuma had not reduced but increased his power; he had let him ally himself with Mexico's only

dangerous enemy. No. Had Montezuma wanted to destroy
him, he would have attacked him in overwhelming force before
Xocotla, as he came out of the desert, exhausted and starving.
The only explanation was that, though he did not want him to
come to the city, yet he would let him come. He had not
wanted him to leave the coast, but when he left it, he acquiesced. Now again he would give in. Yet it was not possible
to be sure without knowing more of his mind. There was nothing for it but to go on and find out. But for him to march on the
capital in a warlike manner would be to throw away the chance
that Montezuma would receive him as the envoy whom he had
always represented himself to be. The Mexican emissaries were
still waiting for their answer. He would give a diplomatic
answer. He would repeat what he had said from the beginning:
that he was an emissary of Charles V and had a message to
deliver, that he came in peace, that he had benefits to bestow.
For Montezuma this answer was as cryptic as all the rest. He
knew Cortés was not an envoy; he knew he was an avenging god.

In his letter to Charles, Cortés relates that the Mexican envoys now suggested that he should let them take him twenty
miles down the road to Cholula, one of Montezuma's vassal
towns, where it would be easier to discuss the question of going
on to the capital, distant thence about sixty miles. He agreed
to this and sent for the lords of Cholula. When they came, he
left Tlaxcala. The difficulty was to get rid of the Tlaxcalans,
who wished to send their whole army with him. But to arrive
at Cholula supported by a host of armed Tlaxcalans would contradict his claim that he was coming in peace. Nevertheless, he
was obliged to start with the army. On getting within six miles
of Cholula, however, he induced it to return, except for 6,000
men who continued with him to the outskirts, where he told
them to remain and not to enter the city. The Tlaxcalans
begged him to be careful; to enter Cholula with his small force
was to put himself in Montezuma's power. They alleged a plot;
Montezuma was enticing him there with evil intent. They had,

of course, the strongest reasons to discourage him from coming to an arrangement with their hereditary enemy.

Cortés was a little shaken by their warnings. Perhaps there was a plot. He entered the town much on his guard, though the people seemed extremely friendly. His immediate plans are well summed up in Bernal's plain words: 'We planned to stay there until we could decide how to get to Mexico without having to fight for it, for the great power of the Mexicans was a fearful thing.'

₡11₿

Cortés at Cholula

Cholula, subject to Montezuma but having its own government, was a large market town, even larger than Tlaxcala. Cortés says it had 20,000 houses, with suburbs of the same magnitude. Without accepting such high figures, we can see that it was certainly the seat of a considerable population. Montezuma did not maintain a garrison there, though he had troops in a town twelve miles to the south. Hundreds of its pyramid temples were to be seen, particularly the immense temple of Quetzalcoatl, which was larger than the Great Pyramid in Egypt. Its reputation as a holy city and the presence in the neighbourhood of Mexican troops sufficed to protect it against its aggressive neighbour, Tlaxcala.

Though Cortés had been invited to enter the city, it was disturbing for the Cholulans that the main army of Tlaxcala had followed him to within six miles and that 6,000 of them were camped just outside the walls. As a precaution, they presently asked the Mexican troops to move up from their garrison to a position close to the city on its west side. They also blocked some of the streets, dug concealed pits with spikes in them, and laid in a supply of stones, which were piled on the flat roofs at strategic points. The women and children were sent out of the city.

These precautions made Cortés suspicious. Were they directed against a possible Tlaxcalan attack or were the Cholulans preparing to fall on him under instructions from Mexico? It was very difficult to tell. 'I was somewhat perplexed,' he wrote later to the Emperor. There seemed to him no reason why the Cholulans should change from friendliness to hostility, unless, as the Tlaxcalans alleged, they had been told to be friendly in order to lure the Spaniards out of Tlaxcala into Montezuma's power. On the face of it this was possible, but by no means certain considering his attitude hitherto. One was back again at the question—what was really in Montezuma's mind? Thanks to Sahagún, the nature of his thought has been, at least, partially revealed, and the reader has been given a glimpse of it. But Cortés had not this key nor had any of his companions who have left a record. Sahagún, who made an intensive study of Mexican sources immediately after the conquest, declares there was no plot, as Montezuma neither then nor at any time contemplated using force to prevent the visit he so much dreaded. The Cholulans, too, did not possess an army adequate for such an attempt.

But the Spaniards grew increasingly suspicious and believed their lives were in danger. Disquieting rumours reached them. The Totonac aides, of whom little mention has been made since the expedition started but who throughout the journey had given steady service, whispered to Cortés that the Cholulans had sacrificed human victims with a ritual that suggested they were about to fight. Doña Marina, too, came forward with a story that the wife of a high officer in the Cholulan forces had secretly warned her of danger and offered her asylum. This information, vouched for by his faithful Marina, convinced Cortés. He became suddenly alarmed and decided to forestall the alleged plot by taking drastic measures. He seems to have thought that the Cholulans would either attack him where he was in the town and call in the Mexicans to help them, or that when he resumed his march to Mexico he would be ambushed in defiles outside, where the Mexicans were waiting. Appar-

ently some informers had told him the first and others the
second rumour.

Having decided to strike before he was struck, his invariable
practice in an emergency, his first step was to summon the chief
lords on the plea that he wanted to discuss his departure. They
all came. That they did so is an argument in favour of their
innocence; had they been plotting they would hardly have been
so incautious as to place themselves in his hands. Without
giving them opportunity to say a word, he seized, bound and
locked them up. At Cempoalan he had threatened to kill the
fat lord unless he told his archers to disperse. In the present
case he did not try to force the imprisoned lords to disband the
troops which, as he supposed, they had in readiness to use
against him. What he intended was to strike immediate terror.
At a pre-arranged signal his men set on the crowd of porters,
guides, followers and the like (armed or not is uncertain), who
were lounging in his courtyard, laughing, as he thought, in a
suspicious manner. After cutting them down he sallied into the
streets and calling in the 6,000 Tlaxcalans waiting outside
'scoured the city', to quote from his letter to the Emperor,
'during five hours until I had forced all the people out of it. We
did such execution that more than three thousand persons
perished.' This was exactly what the Tlaxcalans had hoped for.
They went home laden with loot.

Historians have taken opposing views of this episode. Some
have believed there really was an arrangement between Montezuma and his vassals of Cholula to exterminate the Spaniards.
Having discovered it, Cortés' only hope of saving himself from
destruction was to terrorize the city. Other historians have seen
insufficient evidence of a plot, and think it likely that the Tlaxcalans, who were longing to loot Cholula, deceived Cortés by
feeding him with rumours through people he trusted; in fact,
that it was not a Cholulan but a Tlaxcalan plot. Others again
think that Cortés and his men deceived themselves. Their
nerves had been sorely tried. They did not know precisely how

Montezuma viewed them. Apparently he was well disposed, but might he not at any change his mind? Bernal, who is a most honest chronicler of events as he saw them, thought Montezuma had changed his mind. He writes that some Cholulan priests reported that he consulted the Humming Bird and the Smoking Mirror and was directed by them to use force. But the same writer admits that at the time the question whether the plot had real existence remained in debate and became later a subject for inquiry.

We cannot hope to decide a matter left undecided so long ago. I have adopted what I think to be the explanation which goes best with the whole picture. The precautions taken (and rightly taken) by the Cholulans against their enemies, the Tlaxcalans, were misinterpreted by Cortés. He showed his dark side and demanded victims, so that he might live and carry out his historical mission.

Further back, I described the great festival of Quetzalcoatl when a young man was sacrificed that the god might live. The reader may not remember that Cholula was the town where it took place. Cholula was the city of Quetzalcoatl. He was its divine guardian. In the legendary past when he took human form he lived there and was driven thence by the enraged Smoking Mirror. Victims, besides the youth who annually personified him, were sacrificed to him on occasions when astro-magically his position was weak. Their blood was thought necessary for him if he was to continue to guard the city, though he himself had declared human sacrifice unnecessary. Now came his second appearance as Cortés. Cortés too demanded victims. The parallelism of his massacre with the sacrifices was not lost upon the inhabitants. They knew, everyone knew, that Montezuma had hailed Cortés as the returning god. They saw him arrive with his strange weapons, his stranger beasts, himself pale and bearded as in the legend. What would he do in this, his city? In October 1519 Quetzalcoatl was not astro-magically weak, but he was in a malevolent aspect, as Evening Star. So, when Cortés slaughtered them, it was not surprising. After the massacre the imprisoned lords were set free and called the people back into the city. They returned at once, and went quietly about their business in the markets, happy that the god was no longer angry with them.

Cortés preached the new religion. The people could not understand it. It seemed so different from the old; and to have no connection with their worship of Quetzalcoatl. The god was not even mentioned by name. (Cortés, in fact, did not know his name nor that it was with him that he was identified, though it is clear from Bernal they all knew of Quetzalcoatl's great temple, and of the special reverence in which he was held.) When told by Cortés to destroy the images of all the gods, the Cholulans promised to do it but asked for time. Meanwhile they cleaned one temple and placed a cross in it. And they agreed to open the cages where many men and women were being fattened for sacrifice and let them return to their homes. To obey was painful and disturbing, but since Cortés was the god, they feared him and obeyed. It can never have occurred to them that they had been overawed by a mortal like themselves.

To suppose that Montezuma's mind wavered at this time is not to understand the grounds of his belief in Cortés' identity. That after recognizing him as Quetzalcoatl and passively acquiescing in his march inland, he now designed to trap and kill him as if he were a mortal, is irreconcilable with the nature of the prophecy that foretold Quetzalcoatl's second coming. The prophecy was an astrological calculation translated into mythological terms. In its astrological form it declared no more than that on the 22nd of April in the year 1519 a being would come from the east to destroy the old institutions and rule over the country. In its mythological form the being becomes Quetzalcoatl. The astrological prediction was proved correct. The being, Cortés, landed in the year and on the day foretold with the intentions foretold, and was seen week by week putting his intentions into practice. The mythological side of the prophecy was the explanation of these facts in terms which fitted into the Mexican order of ideas. For Montezuma to have accepted the astrological prediction, but to have rejected its mythological explanation, would have been to discard science as it was understood in his world. Once convinced of the truth of the astrological prophecy by the visible fact of Cortés' appearance at the prescribed time, he was obliged to identify him with Quetzalcoatl. He could no more deny that Cortés was the god than he could deny that Cortés was there. To suppose that his mind wavered at this time and that he doubted Cortés' divinity is to suppose the impossible. To take an opposite analogy, he could not have taken the arrival of Cortés as a natural event any more than an astronomer of to-day could take an eclipse he had predicted as a supernatural event.

So far, Montezuma has been but a shadowy presence off stage. I have called him a haunted creature; I have called him a monster, though religious monster had been a closer definition. Must Cortés also be termed a religious monster, after we have seen him put three thousand to the sword to save his mission from failure? At the start he seemed to us a bright adventurer of the Renaissance, ambitious to win an immortal renown. But he has become more mysterious, more monstrous, more mystical. Well, these two monsters are about to meet. In the next chapter they come face to face. Reeking with the blood of his sacrifices, Montezuma will issue from his palace and advance supported by his sages and princes in ritual procession to the rencontre. We shall see his dress, his features, hear his voice as in lines of great beauty he welcomes the armoured visitant, drenched too in the blood of victims, put to death that the Cross might enter.

⟨12⟩

Montezuma and Cortés Meet

In any normal country an intruder who entered and massacred its inhabitants would be set upon by the sovereign's troops, particularly when the national forces had the advantage of situation and numbers, and were in no way lacking in courage, as in the present case. But in the fantastic world of Mexico this did not happen. Though the massacre at Cholula was the most gross affront to Montezuma, he did not take it amiss nor think it inconsistent with the interpretation he had given to Cortés' apparition. He did not change his mind and attack the aggressor. Cortés was still the advancing god. He had been angered at Cholula. The people, though instructed to welcome and supply him, had incurred his displeasure. They had paid the penalty. To restore him to good humour, Montezuma sent another embassy.

Bernal describes how it arrived. It was led by six lords and carried a present of gold and jewellery worth two thousand pieces-of-eight and several man-loads of very rich mantles. On coming before Cortés the leading envoy said, after touching the ground and lifting the dust to his lips: 'Our Lord the great Montezuma, sends this present to you, Malintzin, with affectionate regards. He much regrets that the Cholulans have annoyed you. They are tiresome people and you have not punished them enough. Count on his friendship. He invites you to the capital. Come when you like and he will do his best to entertain you. I am instructed to guide you by the shortest route. Food and drink will be provided at the stopping places.'

When this was duly translated to Cortés through Doña Marina and Aguilar who by this time, says Bernal, had become very expert, he embraced the envoys. It seemed almost too good to be true. He had got his invitation at last. He would not have to try and fight his way in.

But Montezuma's permission to come on was a manœuvre, as will shortly appear, to entangle Cortés in a magical net. Inside the valley he would be more exposed to the full force of such devices.

Though Cortés had no notion of the real reason for the invitation, he did not banish entirely from his mind the possibility of a military feint. Queer rumours began to circulate, invented perhaps by the Tlaxcalans, who wanted to frighten Cortés into taking their army with him. The Mexicans had been raiding for a hundred years; what a wonderful opportunity to raid them back! The most alarming rumour was that Montezuma had shut himself up with his chief priests for two days and consulted his god of war, the Humming Bird. The advice he received, through mediums or auguries, was that he should entice the Spaniards into his spider's web of a fortress, raise the bridges on the causeways so that they could not escape, starve them and then capture them with his vastly more numerous forces. As this was quite feasible, it made the story all the more unnerving. 'Don't go without us,' pleaded the Tlaxcalans. 'We will gladly place ten thousand picked troops at your disposal.'

But Cortés, though lately so convinced of Montezuma's treachery that he had felt justified in massacring three thousand Cholulans, refused to accept the Tlaxcalans' offer. 'I will take a thousand of your porters and labourers, that is all,' he said. The Tlaxcalans were dumbfounded. Had he altered his opinion about Montezuma's treacherous designs? The Spaniards would never emerge alive from Mexico. After Montezuma had overcome them, their hearts would be cut out and offered to the Humming Bird in the quauhxicalli (the Eagle-dish).

But Cortés was not moved. He sent what Bernal calls 'an affectionate reply' to Montezuma and informed him that he was starting off at once. The Tlaxcalans gave in. Only a god would dare to do such a thing, and he was a god. Perhaps it would turn out right. But he ought to remember that he had to cope not only with the great Montezuma but with his old enemy, the Smoking Mirror, who in Quetzalcoatl's last incarnation had driven him out. It would be a war of gods. And, indeed, that was the truth.

A commander who refused an offer of 10,000 men in such a situation of danger and uncertainty, would normally be thought mad. But Cortés' decision was in keeping with his policy from the first. He never contemplated storming Mexico. He always planned to get there by a strategem. Though his real intentions were not peaceful, he had consistently represented them to be so. It was impossible, therefore, for him to advance on Mexico at the head of 10,000 enemy Tlaxcalans without throwing off the mask. He evidently still thought that it would be easier to get to the capital by guile than by force. But having got there, what was he going to do? He had no credentials from Charles V. His demands were ludicrous for an envoy—vassalage and change of religion. The story will show that he found what to do, though it was so daring and extraordinary that one cannot suppose he had thought of it at this time.

When the Totonacs, who had followed him all the way from the coast, learnt of his decision, their hearts failed them. They dared not go to Mexico, even in company with a god. 'You will be quite safe with us,' Cortés told them. But although, says Bernal, 'Doña Marina put it in the most warm-hearted manner' they still declined. The risk was too great, particularly for them, subjects of Montezuma who had refused to pay taxes. On their departure Cortés made them a liberal present and asked them to deliver two loads of rich mantles to the fat lord of Cempoalan, who was in some sort his father-in-law. He also sent a letter to Juan de Escalante with all the news, urging him to finish Vera Cruz and keep on good terms with the local people. None of the Conquistadores asked leave to go back with the Totonacs, not even those who had hesitated before. 'On to Mexico', was the cry. Not one of them doubted that Cortés could do it.

On November 1st they marched away, mounted scouts in front, the cannon next, then the rest of the horsemen and the main body, each man sharply on the lookout, *la barba sobre el ombro*, the beard on the shoulder, as Bernal etches the scene for our eyes. To reach Mexico they had to cross a pass 12,000 feet high between the volcanoes of Popocatapetl (the Mountain that Smokes) and Iztacciuatl (the White Woman) an extinct volcano, both snow mountains of over 17,000 feet which lay twenty miles due west of Cholula. Popocatapetl had become active after a long quiescence shortly before the Spaniards' arrival, an added portent of calamity in Mexican opinion. 'A great volume of smoke came from it day and night, rising to the clouds as straight as a pillar,' wrote Cortés. As they approached they could hear it roaring. With its cap of snow it was a marvellous sight. That night camp was pitched about six miles below the top of the pass. On reaching the top next day they saw the city of their dreams 5,000 feet below. The map gives an idea of the great panorama. They were some twenty miles from the southern shore of the lake, which at that time filled the greater part of the valley. Near its centre was the island on which Mexico itself stood. As they were the best part of forty-five miles from the city, the causeways which connected it with the mainland can hardly have been visible. The lake, which was fifty miles long, was in six compartments, opening out of each other. Round the shores were ten large towns and twenty smaller ones. This secluded valley at the end of the world, surrounded on all sides by high ranges, was densely populated. Though the people all spoke the Nauatl

tongue, they were not all Mexicans. Only the inhabitants of
Mexico city were of that race. The rest were the descendants
of the several North American tribes which, as explained
further back, settled in the valley before the Mexicans arrived.
But all of them were now subject to Montezuma, and the lords
who governed them were related to him.

Bernal says it came on to snow at the top of the pass, blotting
out the view, and continued to snow as they descended. The
crater of Popocatapetl close on their left was belching smoke
and flames. An icy wind moaned in the pine trees. It was a wild
and desolate scene. Never had they felt so far from home. The
enterprise had never seemed so desperate. In their anxiety they
suspected an ambush and at a fork where the Mexican envoys
wished to take them by one road they insisted on going by the
other. At dusk they reached a group of rest-houses, post inns of
a sort for the use of travelling merchants. 'There we got a good
supper but the cold was intense,' says Bernal, though Cortés
says there was a wood fire in each room. These arrangements
for their comfort had been made by the Mexicans. To suspect
them still of treachery began to seem far-fetched. Nevertheless,
Cortés did not relax his precautions. It was impossible to be
sure how the affair would go.

Next morning, November 3rd, they continued the march
down hill. Proceeding at a leisurely pace through Amecameca
and other small towns they did not reach the southern shore of
the lake at Ayotzinco until the 6th. The people flocked to see
them pass and at each stopping place plenty of food was provided for the whole party.

During this descent to lake-level at 7,400 feet Cortés was
met by no less than three sets of emissaries from Montezuma.
The first of these was a magical embassy. Historians are not
agreed as to its exact significance. It was headed by a personage
who was the image of Montezuma and gave himself out to be
the First Speaker. The reader will recall that an embassy led by
a Mexican very like Cortés had come while the Spaniards were

on the coast. The present case was the opposite, but the intention to bewitch was the same. If Cortés-Quetzalcoatl was induced to treat Montezuma's double as though he were Montezuma and was drawn into a conversation, the words of which created an enchantment, he would be prevented afterwards, by force of enchantment, from recognizing the real Montezuma. But unversed in the details of Mexican magic we cannot know exactly the intention. Whatever it was, the attempt fell flat, because Cortés discovered the personation and refused to receive the ambassador.

After his double failed, Montezuma sent out his regular enchanters. What happened to them was very strange; it is recorded in perhaps the most curious scene of Sahagún's curious book. The march of the Conquistadores was in its plain reality as extraordinary an event as has ever happened. But its power as a real story is heightened by non-real touches which ally it with the great poetic drama of antiquity and give it a universal symbolism. Such is the nature of Sahagún's scene. When the enchanters had gone some part of their way and were in a solitary place, they saw coming towards them down the slope a countryman in a loin-cloth with a grass rope wound eight times round his body. He halted in front of them and blocked the path. He was like a drunk man; or was his drunkenness due to fury? He seemed to rise up in the way and said in a hectoring voice: 'What, you have come again! This time what is your errand? What has Montezuma got in his brain? Has he only now come to his senses? His errors, his guilt, his sins, are past counting. He has given the people over to death. He has wrapped them in their shroud.'

The enchanters were appalled by this denouncement. Suddenly terrified, they saw that it was not a drunken rustic they had to do with, but Tezcatlipoca, the Smoking Mirror. In the magical books it was recorded that he had appeared before in just such a guise and foretold the destruction of the Toltecs, the ruling dynasty which had preceded the Mexican. Throwing themselves on the ground, they prayed fervently, as the apparition continued to rant at them. Hastily they piled up a little pyramid of earth, with a bed of grass for him on the top, and begged him to sit there, so that they might offer him their blood. But he would not even look their way. And opening wide his great mouth he cried: 'What good is it your coming here? All is over. The Mexico that was, is no longer and shall never be again. Too late! Too late! Look what is happening!' And he pointed towards the city.

They looked back and saw that all the temples were ablaze, and the priests' houses, all the houses of Mexico. And it was as if a great battle, too, were raging. They became incoherent and out of their wits. Him who had spoken they could see no more.

Choking with horror they hastened to tell their master. The meaning of their vision was plain. The chief of the gods, who in the old days had driven Quetzalcoatl out of the land, was enraged with Montezuma for having let him return. Mad with fury, he was abandoning Mexico to its fate.

When Montezuma was told the news a vast sadness overtook him. He had provoked what he most dreaded, a supernatural conflict. By refusing to fight Quetzalcoatl, he had aroused the jealousy of Smoking Mirror. If Smoking Mirror, chief guardian of the city, withdrew his protection, the cosmic balance would be upset with incalculable results. He fell into a long silence of despair.

At last rousing himself, he said: 'We have swallowed the poison. Nevertheless, some means may yet be found.' But what means? He would try gold again, more gold, a bigger offer. The incarnate god had made it clear that he preferred gold to any gift. If enough gold were offered he might even now, late though it was, turn his face homewards. And Smoking Mirror would forget his anger.

A new embassy was sent. The envoys earnestly begged Cortés not to come nearer, offering him for himself alone, if he went back, four loads of gold, that is two hundred pounds' weight, and for each captain fifty pounds' weight. But Cortés replied that he must see and talk to Montezuma, in order to explain why he had come. When he had done so, he would depart, if Montezuma did not wish him to remain.

This promise was at least a straw of hope. If the god were paying him but a brief call, there was less reason for alarm. Smoking Mirror could perhaps be appeased; the future might not be as dark as feared. Montezuma felt he had gained a point. It remained for him to welcome the god in a fitting manner. He could do no more for the moment. The third embassy was the result of this decision.

It arrived early in the morning of the 7th while the Spaniards were at Ayotzinco on the south shore of the lake. At the head of it was Cacamatzin (Lord of Small Maize Cobs), Montezuma's nephew, lord of Tetzcuco, the most important lake town after Mexico. All the previous envoys had been lords, but Cacamatzin's rank was far higher. Though quite young, only twenty-five, he was a leading figure in the valley. The ceremony that surrounded him as he approached greatly impressed the watching Spaniards. 'He rode in a litter richly worked in green feathers, with many silver borderings, and rich stones set in bosses made of the finest gold,' Bernal records. Eight lords bore the litter. When Cacamatzin got out, they 'swept the ground and removed the straws where he had to pass'.

Cacamatzin then formally welcomed Cortés and offered to conduct him to the city. He even apologized that Montezuma himself had not come out to meet him. Cortés embraced him and gave him beads.

They all set out at once. Mexico, still twenty miles away, was not visible; it was hidden behind a promontory which, as the map shows, here juts across the lake. But there was much of interest to be seen. They marched along the shore until they reached a preliminary causeway, a broad embankment two miles long which crossed the water to the promontory, not one of the main causeways leading to the city, but a link in the system. Half-way over was an island where stood the town of Cuitlahuac (Place of the Dunged Water), 'the most beautiful we had yet seen,' Cortés told the Emperor, 'not only because of the well-decorated houses and towers, but also for the excellent construction of its foundations in the lake'. Looking west they could see Xochimilco (the Field of Flowers), an island famous for its botanical garden. Having dined well at Cuitlahuac, they continued along the causeway to the promontory and took the road for Iztapalapan (On the Salt-Coloured Water). It was on the far side of the promontory and opposite Mexico, and when they reached it they could see the city's white temples and palaces five miles away, rising from the water of the lake at the end of one of the main causeways. This view of it reminded them of fairy cities in their old romances. 'Some of our soldiers asked whether what we saw were not a dream. I do not know how to describe it all, for we were looking at what had never been heard of or seen before, nor even dreamed about,' says Bernal.

At Iztapalapan they were lodged in a palace, 'spacious and well built, the walls panelled with scented woods, great rooms and courts covered with awnings of cotton cloth'. It was grander than anything they had seen at home. A garden was close by, with paths, flower-beds and bathing-pools, the alleys decorated with carvings in relief. 'No future discoveries will ever be so wonderful. Alas! to-day, all is overthrown and lost, nothing left standing,' sighs Bernal. This sigh, coming from an old Conquistador, is very revealing. As a human being, he could not help regretting the destruction wrought by his countrymen. Thinking of Iztapalapan and the view of Mexico in the midst of the waters, he forgets for a moment that this beauty was only one aspect of Mexican life. Gardens, lily ponds, bathing-pools, sculptured terraces they had indeed, but down the steps of the white towering pyramids, which looked so beautiful from a distance, was oozing, on closer view, streams of blood.

The 8th of November dawned, the day ever memorable, disastrous, epochal, when the Spaniards entered Mexico, or, as it was then called, Tenochtitlan (The Foundation of Stone Prickly Pear). They had as their conductors not only Cacamatzin, Montezuma's nephew, but also his brother Cuitlahuac, lord of the little causeway town of the same name and also of Iztapalapan. A dense crowd lined the way, staring at the extraordinary strangers with amazement and fear, and also with excitement. Sahagún has a passage which describes the scene through their eyes. 'At the head of the column were four riders, who turned their eyes this way and that, in case of a surprise attack. The dogs ran ahead with their noses on the ground. Next came an ensign carrying a banner, waving it, swinging it round his head. Men-at-arms followed, their swords sparkling, with their shields on their shoulders. Behind was a row of riders with lances, their swords hanging from the hips and bells tinkling on their bridles. The horses neigh and sweat, foam at the mouth, their hooves clatter on the roadway. Then come the men with crossbows on their shoulders and quivers crammed with arrows, in quilted armour, plumes in their casques. Again riders, then the musketeers.'

So they marched along the causeway, which veered west to a junction with a side causeway from the town of Coyuacan (Place of Many Lean Coyotes), and then went north straight on to Mexico. Bernal says that when they found themselves surrounded by the crowds on both sides of the way and in canoes on the lake, (not to speak of their escort, the armed men of the princes Cacamatzin and Cuitlahuac), they felt very nervous, remembering how the Tlaxcalans had warned them to beware of entering Mexico. But there was no threatening sign; the expression on all faces was of awe and respect. More and more lords came to welcome them and kiss the earth.

And now the great moment approached when they were to come face to face with Montezuma. They had passed Xoloc, a fortress on the causeway, when word went round that he was on his way to meet them. Cacamatzin and Cuitlahuac hastened ahead. Montezuma had come out of the city and was approaching the head of the causeway. When the princes reached him, he descended from his litter. A canopy of feathers and embroidery was raised and beneath it he walked towards the Spaniards, supported under the arms by the two princes. His mantle was rich, his sandals golden. Ahead of him went other lords, sweeping the ground and spreading cloth as a carpet for his feet. All the lords were barefoot and, except the two who supported his arms, had their eyes lowered in reverence.

'As we approached each other,' wrote Cortés, 'I dismounted and was about to embrace him, but the two lords in attendance prevented me with their hands, so that I might not touch him.'

Bernal says the princes prevented the embrace because they thought it an indignity. But since Montezuma believed Cortés to be a divine incarnation and came afoot to receive him, the objection to the embrace could not have been that it was thought too great a liberty. What the objection was, we cannot tell, but may well suppose it was prompted by fear. Ever since Montezuma had heard of Cortés' arrival, he had been terrified at the idea of meeting him. He could not have imagined that the god would immediately seek to embrace him. The two princes may have read into Cortés' gesture a magical intention. However, they rapidly recovered from their fright and did not object when Cortés took off a necklace he was wearing of multicoloured beads strung on a gold cord scented with musk and hung it round Montezuma's neck.

Montezuma now formally bade Cortés welcome. Sahagún has recorded the beautiful speech and we may be sure that it accurately represents the gist of what was heard by the Mexicans who stood by on that day. A phrase or two of it is found in Bernal, who remembered that much of Doña Marina's translation.

Says Sahagún: 'Montezuma straightened himself to his full height and standing close before Cortés addressed him thus: "O Lord, our Lord, with what trouble, what fatigue, have you journeyed to reach us, have arrived in this land, your land, your own city of Mexico, to sit on your mat, your stool, which I have been guarding for you this while. Your vassals, the old kings, my ancestors, are gone, after they too had kept ready your mat. Would that one of them could rise from the dead and, astonished, see what my eyes truly see, for in no dream do I see your face. Ah, these days, five, ten, a string of days, I have been anxious, watching for you, waiting to see you appear from your hidden place among the clouds and mists. For the kings, my ancestors, told that you would appear, that you would return to sit on your mat, your stool. Now it has come true; you have returned. With toil, with weariness, you have reached us at last. Welcome to this land. Rest now. You are tired. Rest awhile. Rest in your palace. With your companions, the lords, take your rest." '

Who can say how Doña Marina and Aguilar rendered intelligible this lyrical address, thrilling with hidden anguish, humble and adoring? Indeed, we cannot suppose that Cortés received more than a hint of its pathos and renunciation. Even now we can only with difficulty catch its overtones. One of the strangest utterances ever recorded, its ultimate meanings still escape us. We do not know in what consultations, political and priestly, Montezuma had spent the previous day. But evidently he had discovered no way of escaping his fate. He must submit, whatever might come.

Cortés' reply was polite. He expressed no astonishment at the offer of the throne. Perhaps he did not believe it was seriously meant. But the offer of the throne was meant; at least it was an acknowledgment of Cortés' right to the throne. It has to be remembered that Quetzalcoatl was not only a god but that he had, during his last appearance, been King of the Toltecs. He was therefore not only a returning god but a returning king. And a returning Toltec king was, in Mexican opinion, senior to a reigning Mexican king. Cortés reiterated what he had always said—that he came in peace, there was nothing to fear, that he had been longing to see Montezuma, had much to tell him.

Montezuma now announced that he would escort the Spaniards to the house which he was placing at their disposal. A procession was formed, Montezuma walking in front to show the way. They went up a broad street into the heart of the city, watched by an immense crowd. Presently a man came with a parcel. It contained a necklace of golden shrimps that Montezuma had sent for and which he hung round Cortés' neck. If, as is supposed, the necklace was part of Quetzalcoatl's insignia, the gift showed that nothing in Cortés' appearance or speech was thought inconsistent with his being the god.

When they reached the centre of the town, they came to a group of splendid buildings. On their right was Montezuma's immense palace and nearly opposite was the enclosure in which rose up the great pyramid-temple of the Humming Bird. A short distance further on, beside a zoo, was the palace of Montezuma's late father, Axayacatzin (Face of Water Lord), a previous First Speaker. This was the residence where the Spaniards were to stay. Montezuma led them into a great hall and taking Cortés by the hand made him sit by him on a dais. Dinner would soon be ready, he said. They must make themselves at home. As soon as they had eaten and rested, he would visit them again. With these words he left and went to his own palace. 'A splendid dinner came up and we ate it at once,' says Bernal. 'Such was our lucky and daring entry into the great city of Mexico on 8th November 1519. Thanks to our Lord Jesus Christ for it all.'

${13}$

Montezuma Converses with Cortés

It has been hard enough to give a consistent explanation of the extraordinary circumstances which enabled Cortés to reach Mexico. What follows now is still more extraordinary and so the harder to get clear. Yet it flows from what has already been said. Let me recapitulate the main factors, as Montezuma saw them. Firstly, he was convinced, as a modern astronomer would be of a known comet's return, that Quetzalcoatl as prophesied had returned. Quetzalcoatl was an ancient god and part of the universal process. He could not be resisted without endangering the universe. He had had to be offered the kingdom. The result might be great tribulation but would have to be borne. The other gods might take it ill. Smoking Mirror had already shown his anger. But they could perhaps be placated. Quetzalcoatl, it was to be hoped, would act towards them with discretion. A war among the gods would be total ruin. It might still be possible to persuade Quetzalcoatl to go away. The god had already hinted that he came only on a visit. This was, however, to take a comparatively bright view of what was a very menacing situation. Quetzalcoatl's old declaration that he would return, coupled with the disastrous portents recently seen, pointed to the doom of the old order and, in the process, the ruin of the Mexicans. But while there was a glimmer of hope, Montezuma refused to accept doom as certain.

Cortés' point of view has also to be kept clear. Uppermost in his mind was his ambition to conquer Mexico and become its Viceroy under Charles V. Such a conquest would give him vast renown, unlimited riches and great power, three things he desired above all else. He had advanced steadily towards his goal. Taking advantage of Spanish municipal usage, he had discarded his superior, Velázquez, and turned himself into the leader of an expedition to take possession for Charles V of territories whose title the Pope had given to Spain. He had already renamed Mexico New Spain. It followed that its religion could not be other than Catholicism. Had the Mexican religion been a mild and wise creed like Buddhism, it would still have had to be destroyed. That it had deeply shocked him by its human sacrifices was an added incentive to put an end to it, but was not the reason for doing so. He had as yet received no authorization from Charles V, but was satisfied that his legal position was sound. Though he was bent on the complete overthrow of Mexican independence and civilization, Montezuma had welcomed him and declared the country to be his. But he had not conquered the country. The alarming truth was that he was inside a fortress in the middle of a lake in the middle of a remote kingdom, with a handful of soldiers and no secure line of communications. He was entirely at the mercy of those whose ruin it was his ambition to compass. If they were deceiving him or if they changed their mind, he was lost. How did one conduct oneself in a situation so paradoxical that it had no precedent in the whole of history? In the realm of reason there was no answer to this question. But Cortés was not perturbed. Crafty, methodical, careful, he was also, as I have suggested, a man with a mystical confidence in his star. He was fated to win; he was the instrument of divine providence. So far he had come unscathed; somehow or other he would get through to the end. Only this sublime certainty could have nerved him to take the astonishing measure which will be described in the next chapter.

For the moment we must look about us, as the Spaniards were doing. The palace in which they were lodged consisted of a number of stone buildings dressed with lime and polished till they glittered. The rooms were numerous and large, hung with painted cottons and very clean. There were courtyards, baths, fountains, gardens. Outside, the city stretched away on all sides. They had had a glimpse of it as they came in; the houses of volcanic stone, with flat roofs; the streets like those of Amsterdam or Venice, half-roadway, half-canal; bridges everywhere; palaces and temple-pyramids wherever you looked. It was, in fact, one of the largest and most beautiful cities in the world. Its length was about as far as from Oxford Circus to St. Paul's; its breadth was about two-thirds of its length. The altitude of 7,400 feet made the air invigorating. The Spaniards found their energy renewed. After years in the islands and their stay on the relaxing coastal belt, the change was a tonic; they felt ready for anything.

As Montezuma had promised, he was back again soon after dinner was finished. 'He came to our quarters in the greatest state,' says Bernal, 'accompanied by numerous lords, all of them his kinsmen.' He looked not more than forty, though he was fifty-two years old. 'He was of good height and well proportioned, slender and spare of body, his complexion the average brownness of his people. He did not wear his hair long but so as just to cover his ears. His black beard was thin and well shaped. Though his face was long it was cheerful; his eyes were good and his expression tender and grave. He was very neat and clean.'

It is not the least complicating factor in an already nearly incomprehensible situation that the Spaniards greatly admired Montezuma and grew fond of him. Though he was a ritual murderer on a big scale and a cannibal, Bernal even got the impression that he was very devout. He always calls him the

Great Montezuma and repeats more than once that he had the air and gestures of an accomplished prince, a phrase which at that time had a definite meaning. Bernal's simplicity allowed him to feel that Montezuma was the protagonist in a gigantic drama, but try as he would he could not enter into his thought. Again and again he apologizes for his shortcomings as a writer; the theme was so splendid, his resources so small.

Cortés went to meet Montezuma as he entered. They shook hands. Seats were brought and they began to converse. Montezuma introduced the burning subject—Cortés' identity. He told him plainly that he believed him to be the person long foretold who 'would come from the sunrise and rule over these lands'. It was as if he wished Cortés to confirm his belief. It was certainly the opening gambit in a conversation to find out what Cortés intended to do. Cortés seemed to him more genial than he had dared to hope. Perhaps the affair would not go as badly as he had feared.

Cortés replied that it was true he had come from the sunrise. He said nothing about being the divinity whom Montezuma believed him to be, though he did not directly deny it. He fell back on the explanation of his coming which he had put out from the first. He was the subject of a great Emperor called Charles V. News of Montezuma had come to Charles's ears. He, Cortés, had been sent to beg Montezuma to become a Christian. What exactly that meant and how it could be effected he would explain later. This statement was fictitious. He had not been sent. But he hoped that it would turn out partly true. By this time Charles V had got the letters from Vera Cruz. A royal authorization to annex and Christianize Mexico might arrive any day.

But what meaning could Montezuma attach to a statement that Quetzalcoatl was an envoy from an emperor? This is a difficult question to answer. Yet it has to be answered if what follows is to make sense. Montezuma is unlikely at first to have thought of Charles V as an earthly sovereign. Had he done so, he would have asked Cortés for his written credentials or at least for some proof that he was Charles's envoy. And he would have demanded to know where Spain was and all about it. But he asked none of these questions. On page 99 I touched on this problem and suggested there that the Tlaxcalans, when told of Charles V, may have associated him with the supreme deity called The Two. Montezuma must also have been acquainted with the story, referred to on that page, of Quetzal-coatl receiving instructions from The Two before descending to earth. He may not, however, have given that interpretation to what Cortés said. There were other possible interpretations. Charles V may have seemed to him no more than another aspect of Quetzalcoatl himself. Just as in Christianity you have the concept of the Trinity, Three in One, so in Mexican mythology there would be no difficulty in conceiving of the two, Cortés and Charles V, as being also the one, Quetzalcoatl. Though we cannot be sure of the exact category of divine persons in which Montezuma may have placed Charles, it can be assumed that, since all his science told him that Cortés was a divine incarnation, he thought of Charles, to begin with, as more than a human ruler. When therefore in reply he declared himself ready to acknowledge Charles as his sovereign lord, his words should be taken in that sense. He kept silent about the new religion. That, indeed, was a difficulty he must have felt might be insuperable. To neglect the gods of Mexico would be to invite a cosmic catastrophe.

Bernal tells us that politeness did not permit too long and wearisome a conversation on this first occasion. After Montezuma had distributed presents of gold, jewellery and mantles to all the Spaniards, and given orders that food and fodder should be supplied daily, and women sent to grind maize, he took his departure.

Before going to bed Cortés posted his cannon at points along the high wall which surrounded the palace and set a watch. He was taking no risks. He could not tell what might happen. His reception might be a ruse, as his Tlaxcalan allies had warned him. Or Montezuma might change his mind. Or the great lords of the other cities on the lake, almost as large as Mexico city, might not share their master's views.

The night passed without incident. At dawn in the great temple opposite the Spanish quarters the priests began the daily sacrifice of cock quails, without whose blood the sun-god, Tonatiuh, would not have the strength to rise. The Mexican cock quail was a black bird speckled with white, a symbol of the starry night. That the night should die and let the sun rise was magically assisted by the death of the quails. Human sacrifice was also performed at this hour. The Spaniards were so placed as to be able to see blood running down the steps of the pyramid. They could also hear the roaring of the carnivora in the zoo close by, which were fed on the bodies of those sacrificed to the gods, only the limbs being cooked and served at table. The palace of Lord Face of Water between the temple and the zoo was a frightening spot for anyone with weak nerves.

As soon as he got up, Cortés sent a message to Montezuma to say that he was coming to return his call. He set out soon afterwards with Alvarado, Sandoval and two other captains, and a guard of five soldiers, including Bernal. Montezuma received them in his private apartments, a great saloon with a carved wooden ceiling, the walls faced with jasper and porphyry, and hung with embroideries and feather-work. The conversation soon turned to the question of religion. Cortés did not mince matters. It was essential, he said, for Montezuma to understand that his declaration of willingness to acknowledge Charles V as his political sovereign obliged him also to accept him as his spiritual guide. To call himself the vassal and friend of His Most Christian Majesty but refuse to embrace Christianity was a fatal contradiction. His present religion was a horrible delusion. To this Montezuma replied that the Mexican explanation of the universe was old and had been found to work.

In proof of this he pointed out that Cortés (one of their gods) had appeared in the year and on the day when it had been calculated by their divine science that he would appear.

The conversation ended in deadlock. It was clear that Montezuma was not inclined to discuss religion further. 'Do not trouble to speak to me any more about it at present,' he concluded, according to Bernal. So as not to appear importunate, Cortés now took leave, saying that he must not keep Montezuma from his lunch, for it was already past midday. Before the Spaniards left, Montezuma again distributed among them presents of gold, jewellery and mantles. This won their hearts. On the way back they spoke with admiration of his wonderful generosity. 'We must all be sure always to take off our hats to him,' they said.

For the next two days Cortés did not leave his quarters in Lord Face of Water's palace. His situation was very peculiar, so peculiar as hardly to be put into plain words. The main fact was clear enough. Montezuma, though a more powerful and splendid monarch even than he was depicted by the coast people, had professed himself ready to resign to him the government. He had installed him in a grand palace and lavished gifts on him. But it was not so clear what he would do next. How would he put his declarations into practice? So far nothing had been done. He, Cortés, was no more than an honoured guest. How could he actually get control of what had been declared his? He had tested Montezuma's sincerity by urging a change of religion and had met with a refusal. The truth was that he was powerless. But was that really true? Had he not a hold over Montezuma? Was not the prophecy enough to give him a hold? Montezuma's refusal to discuss religious subjects suggested that he had no hold. But everything else suggested that he had. He recalled how at first Montezuma had refused to let him come, but had given way for unexplained reasons. It had paid to come on regardless of risk. It might pay again to press what demands he thought essential. The religious change-over—the best way of breaking up the Mexican government which was a kind of theocracy—could be done gradually, as the ecclesiastics with him advised, done the way he did it *en route* from the coast, when the Virgin was installed in one of a city's temples. That was one demand he could make and others would occur to him. If his demands were met, he would have ground to believe that Montezuma's fantastic declaration was true, and bit by bit he would get control of the country. If they were not met, he should be able at least to leave Mexico loaded with gold, judging from the way they were now treating him. But first of all he ought to reconnoitre the city.

So on November 12th, four days after his arrival, he sent a message to Montezuma saying that he would like to go to Tlatelolco (The Round Earthwork), as the northern quarter of the city was called, and have a look at its two great sights, its market and its great pyramid temple, which was slightly higher than the one opposite his quarters. Montezuma raised no objection and a party of Spaniards, fully armed, set out, guided by lords sent to escort them.

The size of the market surprised them. Thousands of people were buying and selling. Order was kept by police. In one part they saw dealers in jewels and the precious metals. In another slaves were up for sale. Here were the cloth merchants, there the sellers of piece goods. You could buy chocolate, sandals, ropes, skins. Food in abundance was on the stalls—vegetables, turkeys, rabbits, dogs. And pottery in a thousand forms from water jars to little jugs. Bernal's list runs on for pages. What struck him most of all were the public conveniences, for at that time such things did not exist in Spain.

Leaving the market the Spaniards entered the precincts of the temple which was dedicated both to the Humming Bird and the Smoking Mirror, that is to the senior deity, and his aspect as war god. The court in front of it, says Bernal, was larger than the Plaza of Salamanca where Cortés had learnt his law. Montezuma himself was waiting for them on top of the pyramid, for he had gone ahead to kill some boys, so as to keep the two gods in a good temper. On seeing Cortés below he sent down priests to help him up the 114 steep steps, but Cortés would not let the sinister creatures touch him and made his own way to the platform on the summit, as big as a small plaza, as Bernal describes it. On it were the buildings which housed the gods. These were curtained. In front of them were sacrificial stones drenched with human blood.

They found Montezuma in a charming mood; he took Cortés' hand and invited him to admire the view. The whole city was spread below. 'That huge and cursed temple stood so high,' says Bernal, 'that we could see the causeways that led across the lake, the causeway of Iztapalapan by which we had entered, the north causeway to Tepeyacac and the causeway of Tacuba by which we were to flee on the night of our defeat.' The voices of the people in the market could be distinctly heard. The lake stretching away to the cities on its banks was crowded with canoes. They could also see the aqueduct which carried the city's water supply from the mainland at Chapultepec (In the Hill of the Grasshopper).

Cortés now asked to be shown the interior of the buildings on the platform. Montezuma hesitated, but after consulting his priests let the Spaniards enter the shrines of the dread duality. The two were monstrous with terrible eyes, all covered with precious stones in a mosaic, girdled with snakes and with necklaces of silver hearts. Below them were human hearts, freshly plucked from living victims. 'The walls of the oratory were so splashed and encrusted with blood that they were black and the floor was the same. The place stank so abominably that we could hardly wait the moment to get out of it.'

When they were in the open air again, Cortés, assuming a light tone, so as not to offend Montezuma, though he was horror-struck like the rest, said: 'I cannot understand how so great and wise a prince as you can believe that such evil things as these are gods. They are devils.' And he asked leave to put up a cross and an image of the Virgin. On hearing this translated, the priests showed great annoyance and Montezuma was clearly vexed. To put a woman's image in the war-god's temple! 'Had I thought you were going to talk like this,' he said, assuming like Cortés a light tone, 'I would not have shown you over the place.' And he explained shortly that the gods were the powers of nature and that, if nature were to continue to function, the gods must be given their proper nutriment.

Cortés did not pursue the argument. Changing the subject he suggested airily it was time to go home. Montezuma agreed, but said he personally was obliged to stay on and sacrifice a few more people to soothe the Smoking Mirror, after the affront that had been offered him.

The Spaniards climbed down the pyramid and on their way out through the courtyard below saw more horrors. They were shown the room where the dead bodies of victims, rolled down the pyramid after the hearts had been cut out, were collected and cut up, and where the limbs reserved for the priests were cooked. The skull-racks were also shown, a repository where the skulls of all victims were spitted and preserved. 'They were arranged in perfect order,' says Bernal, 'but one could not count them because there were too many.' Opening off the courtyard were two select academies for boys and girls. It was odd to find a high school on such premises. The pupils were being educated, it seemed, with strict care.

This was enough sightseeing for the day. The Spaniards went home, shaken by what they had seen, apprehensive and puzzled.

ℰ14ℬ

Cortés Confines Montezuma

W as Montezuma mad? is one of the questions which this story poses. There is not the smallest evidence that the Spaniards thought him mad. He appeared deluded, and deluded, as some of them conceived, by the Devil who at that time was believed to be a real supernatural person, defeated but still strong enough to oppose God. The opinion that Montezuma was devil-deluded and that the whole Mexican religion was the Devil's invention, was, however, difficult to square with the prophecy which had favoured the invasion. Why should the Devil utter a prophecy whose effect would be to assist those who wanted to destroy his rule in Mexico? The Spaniards had, no doubt, answers to this conundrum, such as that God had forced the Devil to utter a self-destructive prophecy, just as the demons in possessed persons were recorded in the Bible as testifying to Christ's divinity. Those who gave credit to this explanation saw in the prophecy the first step in a divine plan to give them possession of the country. As Cortés believed himself to be the instrument of this divine plan, its further details would presently be revealed. This belief, the product of his personal ambitions moulded by the religious ideas of his time, encouraged him to take risks which common prudence would have told him were too great. Both he and

Montezuma were each in their opposite ways driven by the prophecy.

If it did not occur to the Spaniards that Montezuma was mad, have we any grounds for thinking that he was? Ought we to view him as some kind of a psychopath? Should we ask the psychiatrists to pronounce on him? He was no madder than his predecessors. Take his immediate predecessor, Auitzotzin (Lord Water-opossum). Thirty-two years previously this Mexican sovereign had dedicated the temple of the Humming Bird which stood opposite the Spaniards' quarters and was similar to the one they visited in the northern part of the city. One of the best-established facts of Mexican history is that 20,000 captives were sacrificed on that occasion. They were not all sacrificed at the one temple. That would have been impossible. The 20,000 were probably divided up between the two Humming Bird temples in the metropolis. For twenty days long queues of captives waited below these pyramids to have their hearts cut out. The priests operated till they were exhausted. There were great public banquets of human legs and arms. The carnivora in the zoo were gorged with the trunks. This nightmare orgy was madder than anything done by Montezuma.

The psychiatrists would probably tell us that all the Mexicans were suffering from some kind of mental derangement. They had inherited a religion of fear from earlier civilizations and, instead of growing out of it, had greatly elaborated it and in consequence had grown more frightened. There seemed to be no laughter or compassion left in their character. They had shouldered the grim responsibility of maintaining the cosmic round. Their ruling caste was dedicated to that superhuman task and drenched the altars with blood in their efforts to discharge it efficiently. The Spaniards owed their admission to the country solely to the fact that Cortés was conceived of as an astro-magical force. Each move in the drama was subject to the influence of this fantasy. As long as he was held to be that, and not the leader of an invading force arrived from a country overseas hitherto unknown, he was safe and the profit he might hope to make depended on how successfully he exploited so lucky a chance. But the moment his astro-magical identity was doubted, he would begin to be in danger; if the doubt became general, his position would be that of an ordinary invader.

Cortés, being ignorant of the Mexican system of thought and precluded from finding out its nature, both by the absence of any persons to explain it and his own inability to understand it if they did, could not be quite sure he was safe as long as he did nothing to destroy the illusion which protected him. Despite Montezuma's declarations, he judged himself to be in a precarious position. He had not been invested with any executive functions nor was there any talk that this might follow. It may be that Montezuma, when he said he was ready to hand over the country, did not intend this to have an everyday practical meaning; he would continue in his executive office, while Cortés' authority would be of an astro-magical kind. This possible interpretation never entered Cortés' head. All he saw was that, though his power had been acknowledged, he exercised no functions. He had attempted to exert his powers in the case of religion and had been resisted. Yet something must be done; he could not live in a vacuum. He resolved accordingly on a stroke which, though in fact safe, was dangerous as far as his information went. He decided to put Montezuma under restraint. On the face of it, such an action taken by a man in his position was likely to rouse the Mexicans to fury. Yet he thought it was practicable, partly because his reception was only to be explained on the assumption that the Mexicans credited him with some sort of power which they could not, or ought not to, resist, and partly, as I have explained, because the prophecy was a guarantee of success, inasmuch as it had been inspired by God.

Before he put the plan into execution two events of importance happened. The palace of Lord Face of Water where the Spaniards put up was normally used as a treasury where a large reserve of tribute, gold, jewels, mantles and the like was stored. Among its maze of rooms was a chamber which Montezuma had sealed up. The Spaniards heard a rumour of this and one day when looking for a suitable place to build an altar they saw marks that suggested a hidden door. Chipping off the plaster, they found the entrance to the treasure chamber. Cortés and some of his captains went in first. 'They beheld,' says Bernal, 'such a number of jewels and slabs and plates of gold and jades and other great riches, that they were speechless.' All the soldiers were allowed to have a look. 'I had never seen such riches in my life,' adds Bernal, 'and felt sure there could not be another such store in all the world.' Cortés did not take anything and had the door sealed up as before. But he resolved that the treasure should be his. The sight of the gold had greatly excited his followers. They would risk anything, he reflected, even the seizure of Montezuma, to get it into their hands and safely away.

The second important event was of a very different kind but was also relevant to what he had in mind. It will be recalled that Juan de Escalante had been left to garrison Vera Cruz in the Totonac country. News now came in that he had been killed along with several of his men. The facts were these. The Mexicans had a garrison on the gulf coast about 150 miles north-west of Vera Cruz. Some little time after the Spaniards marched inland, the Mexican governor, a man called Quauhpopoca (Smoking Eagle) told the Totonacs that they must now pay their taxes. They refused and appealed to Escalante for help. He had only forty soldiers fit to fight, two cannon and two muskets fit to fire. However, he sallied out against Quauhpopoca with a supporting force of Totonacs. The Mexicans, who numbered four thousand, defeated him. He managed to get back to Vera Cruz, but died there of his wounds. The result was that the Totonacs submitted to the Mexicans. The garrison at Vera Cruz was beleaguered and in great peril.

On hearing this, Cortés assumed that Quauhpopoca had

acted as he had done under instructions from Montezuma. If our reading is correct, this could hardly have been so; or if Montezuma did tell Quauhpopoca to collect the taxes he did not anticipate that the Spaniards would march out and fight. There is some evidence that he required a Spanish head for magical purposes, but this did not mean any change in his attitude to the Spaniards in general. If, however, Montezuma was responsible in the sense that Cortés believed and was turning against him, an attempt to imprison him would immediately precipitate an attack, which Cortés was very badly situated to meet, as he himself was really the prisoner. But for the reasons I have given and now also because he concieved that the situation could only be righted by a desperate fling, he continued in his resolve to seize Montezuma. There is evidence in Bernal's history that the Spaniards, after five days in a sinister and mysterious city surrounded by hosts of armed Mexicans, were feeling extremely nervous. The news from Vera Cruz alarmed them still more. Thus, Cortés' plans, conceived in the first place as a step towards the practical assumption of the power which had been offered to him, became an attempt to forestall a supposed onslaught on himself.

How the seizure was effected is related by Bernal, who was present, by Cortés himself, and more shortly by a soldier called Andrés de Tapia who was also there. But what passed was at bottom incomprehensible to them. None of them attempted to reconcile Montezuma's behaviour on the occasion with their supposition that he was privy to the attack on the Spaniards at Vera Cruz.

On the morning of November 14th Cortés sent word to Montezuma that he wanted to speak to him about what had happened at Vera Cruz. Montezuma replied that he would be glad to see him. It will be remembered that Montezuma's palace was only some fifty yards down the same street. Cortés, after ordering the main body of his soldiers to stand on the alert inside the quarters, and posting small detachments at the corners of nearby side streets so as to secure his return, walked to the palace with five of his captains, including Alvarado and Sandoval, and a squad of soldiers fully armed. He was admitted into Montezuma's presence. The sovereign's court and large bodyguard were in attendance or within easy call.

After the usual polite exchanges, Cortés put on an angry expression and reproached Montezuma for perfidiously attacking him in Vera Cruz while he protested his friendship in Mexico. Montezuma seemed alarmed by the god's tone. He protested at once that he had not ordered Quauhpopoca to attack the Spaniards. An inquiry would be held, he would send for Quauhpopoca, those responsible would be punished. And calling messengers, he gave them his seal and ordered them to set out immediately for the coast. Cortés thanked him, and then came to the point. Until the matter is cleared up, he said, I would like you to move over to Lord Face of Water's palace.

The request was a great shock to Montezuma. He had feared that troubles were in store for him, but to be made captive was an unexpected humiliation. You are proposing to detain me? he asked. Certainly not, Cortés assured him. All I suggest is that you, your wives, your children, your whole court should come and stay with me. You will be at perfect liberty to leave when you like. You can bring your lords, hold your council, transact state business as usual, have what entertainments and food you please. Any suite of rooms you select will be reserved for you.

That it was a grievous affront and that his lords would never consent, was Montezuma's reply.

No affront is meant, said Cortés. You will be as comfortable there as you are here. My men, who already admire you, will treat you with every respect. You and I will be able to converse with more ease. I have made plans for your advancement. My intention is to support you against your enemies and make you a yet greater sovereign than you are. Your boundaries will be extended with my assistance.

What will my people say! Montezuma could only repeat.

Cortés Confines Montezuma

You must tell your people, said Cortés, that you are going at your own wish. Say your gods have commanded it. That will allay popular excitement and prevent a breach of the peace.

Montezuma still hesitated. He knew that he must submit. Truly, a god had commanded it. The humiliation would have to be borne. There were no magical reasons against his detention as fundamental as those which had nerved him to evade Cortés' demand to put the Virgin's image on the pyramid. But it seemed so hard to endure. To be turned out of his own palace where he had been living for seventeen years! Yet, Quetzalcoatl was the rightful king. He became silent.

Bernal writes that at this point the Captains, thinking that Montezuma was about to order his bodyguard to kill them, cried: 'Stab him if he cries out!' This, however, was a complete misconception. Montezuma had no intention of the sort. After begging Cortés to take his son and two daughters as hostages instead of himself, and being refused, he at last agreed to go. He told the court and the officers of the bodyguard that it was his own wish and that they must respect his wish, for it would be to his advantage. The courtiers heard him with consternation. With grief his lords, barefooted and eyes lowered, brought his litter, and weeping, placed him on it in profound silence. 'Thus we went to my quarters,' wrote Cortés to Charles, 'without causing any commotion in the city, and all was as completely quiet as if nothing had happened.' And Bernal sums up: 'All the attentions and amusements which it was possible for him to have, both Cortés and all of us did our best to afford him. He was not put under any personal restraint and soon all the principal Mexican lords and his nephews came to talk with him and learn the reason of his seizure and whether he wished them to attack us. Montezuma answered them that he was delighted to be some days with us. They must not excite themselves nor the city, nor take it to heart, for what had happened was agreeable to the gods.'

Montezuma as priest-king was the supreme authority on

what was pleasing to the gods. He had, we may be sure, again and again discussed the return of Quetzalcoatl with the High Priest, and with the other two members of his Council of Three, the Governor of the City and the Commander-in-Chief. Like all Mexican noblemen, these two last had in their time been priests and were professors of the sacred lore. Every step he had taken so far must have been in agreement with them. They will have concurred with his reading of the magical books and like him seen no alternative but to submit to the fate foretold for the country. His kinsmen, the rulers of the lake cities, had not the science to contradict him. That he was abandoning his sovereignty seemed to them a terrible thing, but they had no alternative to accepting the fact. Nevertheless, as we shall see, there were some lords who refused to agree.

In a week or so Quauhpopoca and three of his captains arrived in custody from the coast. Cortés had them taken first into Montezuma's apartments. What transpired at that interview is not recorded, but Montezuma sent them to Cortés to be tried. On Quauhpopoca being asked whether he had killed the Spaniards by order of Montezuma, he replied that he had not been ordered to do so. My view is that this must have been true, though under his general orders he had found himself in a situation where to kill Spaniards seemed what was expected of him. Cortés condemned him and his captains to death by burning. The sentence was carried out in the square in front of Montezuma's palace. The fuel used was a quantity of wooden arms collected from the palaces.

By this black and violent deed Cortés let the public see that he had assumed executive functions. And he made his authority yet more explicit by taking the precaution to chain Montezuma during the burning. He now knew how he stood. He had tried out his power and found that he really possessed it. That he did not fully understand Montezuma's motives and tragical dilemma was no matter. He understood enough to know he was safe. From this time he began to get to like Montezuma.

ᕫ15ᕬ

Montezuma Bows to His Fate

With the monarch and his court installed in Lord Face of Water's palace, the Spaniards were able to observe at close quarters the state he kept. The way his meals were served seemed very lavish. At each meal there were thirty courses. The dishes were kept warm over pottery braziers on a side table. Bernal, who knew that Montezuma sometimes ate the flesh of young boys, made a point of looking carefully at the dishes to see if he could detect an arm or a leg, but could never be sure because of the quantities of turkey, pheasant, partridge, quail, duck, venison, wild boar and rabbit which were served. Montezuma sat on a soft low stool at a table which was spread with a white cloth. He always used a napkin and, when he began to eat, a screen was placed so that he could not be seen, except by the women who waited on him and some old lords who stood close behind his seat. With these he conversed and now and then gave them snacks from his plate. His drink was the chocolate they prepared as a stimulant. After dinner he would watch dancers and contortionists, smoke a pipe or cigar, and take a nap. His harem was large, the women beautifully dressed. Cortés encouraged him to maintain the full etiquette of audience. Even the greatest lords were not allowed into his presence until they had covered their embroidered cotton mantles with rough cloaks woven from the cactus leaf.

Montezuma Bows to His Fate

They came in barefoot and did not dare raise their eyes; and they went out backwards, making him obeisances. 'Whenever we passed before him,' says Bernal, 'we doffed our mailed caps. The flattery and attention we paid him and the conversations he had with us gradually made him fairly contented.' In all this Cortés' object was to have him as a puppet ruler, draped in royal splendour but ready to do what he was told.

Montezuma's willingness to serve as Cortés' lieutenant was put to sharp test as time went on. It will be recalled that the most prominent man at court was his nephew, the young Cacamatzin (Lord Maize Cobs), ruler of Tetzcuco, a city on the east shore of the lake. The citizens of Tetzcuco were not Mexicans, but a different clan of the same language group. They had settled by the lake earlier than the Mexicans, and fancied themselves to be more advanced than them, in spite of having become in the previous century their vassals. Lord Maize Cobs, therefore, though his mother was Montezuma's sister, headed a population which did not always see eye to eye with the Mexicans. They had their own ecclesiastical colleges and their own interpretations of the magical books. Prompted, no doubt, by his priesthood, Lord Maize Cobs had not been altogether sure that to resist Cortés would be catastrophic. There is evidence that he advised Montezuma to resist him at the time of the Spanish march on the city. Moreover, it seems, as is explained on a later page (p. 224) that a period of eight days would soon arrive when, astro-magically, it would be an especially propitious moment to attempt to drive Cortés-Quetzalcoatl away. So it was natural that he was less inclined than some others of the lords to look on Montezuma's detention as inevitably fated. An ambitious man, he thought he saw in what amounted to the deposition of the First Speaker an opportunity of making himself First Speaker, thereby raising Tetzcuco to its former position as the leading town in the valley. He hatched a conspiracy with the ruling lords of four of the principal lake cities and secretly assembled a large army. Montezuma's informers brought him the news and he immediately told Cortés. A counter strategem was devised. Lord Maize Cobs was enticed into a Tetzcuco building which stood over the lake. Some canoes full of armed men were moored under the room where he was in conference. He was dragged down into one of them and paddled the fifteen miles across to Mexico. There they carried him in a litter to Lord Face of Water's palace. Cortés did not put him to death but locked him up. A heavy iron chain belonging to the ships had been sent from Vera Cruz and his neck was inserted into one of the links. His accomplices, the ruling lords of the four lake cities, were subsequently arrested and their necks also were put through the chain. Years later when Cortés, become a marquess, was designing his coat of arms he encircled the quarterings with a chain embedded in which were the heads of these deposed rulers. Their suppression was an important step towards his control of the country, for he placed in their stead puppet rulers. The man he appointed to Tetzcuco was Lord Swallow, who became a Christian and took the name of Don Carlos.

We are dealing here with the events which occurred in Mexico city between the seizure of Montezuma on 14th November 1519 and Cortés' departure from the city at the end of April 1520. Their precise order is uncertain, but it seems that soon after the collapse of Lord Maize Cob's conspiracy, which gave Cortés so much firmer a hold on the administration, he decided to call on Montezuma to swear fealty to Charles V. If this were formally done before a notary, his own legal position would be strengthened. He had as yet had no word from the Emperor. His bloodless conquest of Mexico, which he had effected in his capacity as commander of troops entrusted to him by the municipality of Vera Cruz, had received no sanction. But if Montezuma took the oath of allegiance in the proper form, it would be well nigh impossible for Charles to repudiate Cortés and the conquest.

Further back the question was asked what Montezuma

understood when Charles V was mentioned, and various suggested answers were given. With Montezuma in Lord Face of Water's palace, there had been daily conversations between him and Cortés. Sometimes they played gambling games together; sometimes Cortés explained Christianity; sometimes he enlarged on the greatness of Charles. One must suppose that after a while Montezuma got it clear that the Emperor was not Cortés' alter ego, but a distinct personage, the real sovereign of a real country, and probably not a divinity. If he came to that conclusion—and I am forced to believe that eventually he did—we are again confronted with the difficulty of determining how he explained the fact that Cortés, whose identification with Quetzalcoatl he never doubted, alleged himself to be the subject of such a mortal Emperor. Puzzling though this question is, an answer can be found. Quetzalcoatl, during part of his previous incarnation, is represented in the histories as living as a teacher under a Toltec sovereign, whom he later succeeded. Montezuma had precedent, therefore, for supposing him to live now under an earthly sovereign. It became a reasonable explanation that Charles, after profiting by his religious teaching and hearing from him of lands in the far west, where he had once preached before, had sent him back to teach his religion there again. In such a view Charles became the protector of a dispensation which it had been prophesied would come a second time to Central America. As such he was worthy of the greatest respect.

Montezuma accordingly sent for his councillors and sought their agreement to Cortés' request. It may seem strange that councillors who had acquiesced in Montezuma's captivity by Cortés should feel that an open acknowledgment of vassalage to Charles V was any great matter. But here the answer must be that what Montezuma had done so far was to acknowledge a god, while now he was asked to acknowledge a man. Charles in their eyes was less than Cortés.

The lords were much distressed, but found it impossible to

refuse Montezuma. 'They replied that they would do as he had ordered them,' says Bernal, though they could not disguise their bitter grief. The ceremony was fixed for the following day. Cortés' secretary acted as notary. The swearing away of the country's independence was a cruel ordeal for the Mexicans. 'They showed much emotion in doing so and Montezuma could not restrain his tears. He was so dear to us and we were so much affected at seeing him weep, that our own eyes were melting. One soldier wept as openly as Montezuma, such was the affection we had for him.'

This tender scene belongs to high comedy. From the moment the Spaniards had entered the city it had only needed a word from Montezuma to ensure their destruction. But he had never spoken the word, and now rather than speak it submitted to a fate, which he deemed unavoidable, though it was entirely imaginary. So strange a scene contains too many subtleties ever to be entirely comprehensible. We peer at the figures, dimly seen across the centuries. But strain our eyes as we may, something escapes us.

❦16❧

Montezuma's Treasure

As you read Bernal's engaging and simple narrative, written in his extreme old age as he looked back on the fabulous adventures of his youth, the strange fact emerges that he had a warmer feeling for Montezuma than for Cortés. Both he and his companions were really fond of the strange king of the Mexicans. They had several reasons for liking him, but it was his boundless generosity that won their hearts. 'He never omitted giving us every day presents of gold and cloth,' says Bernal. He used to play pitch and toss with gold pellets and 'divided what he won among us soldiers on guard'. Cortés had ordered a Spanish page called Orteguilla to attend him, a clever boy who had picked up enough Nauatl to make himself understood. One day Bernal asked Orteguilla 'to beg Montezuma to do me the favour of giving me a pretty young woman. Montezuma sent for me and said: "They tell me you are in need of cloth and gold and would also like a girl. I will order them to give you one to-day. Treat her well. Her parents are of good family. They will give you cloth and gold." I answered him with great reverence that I kissed his hands for his great favour and might God our Lord prosper him. He asked Orteguilla what I said. On hearing it translated he remarked: "Bernal seems to me to be a gentleman." And he told them to give me in addition three small slabs of gold and two loads of mantles.

The girl was a lady. Her bearing showed it. She was given the name of Doña Francisca.' Bernal makes no further mention of this girl.

Cortés had had two sloops built and launched on the lake. He did this as a precaution in case the causeways were shut against him one day and he were cut off from the mainland. These sloops besides oars had sails, which Mexican canoes had not. When Montezuma heard, he asked Cortés to let him go for an excursion in them to an island which was a royal game reserve. Cortés agreed, though he ordered a guard to accompany him. Montezuma invited a large party of courtiers as well as bringing his huntsmen. He embarked with some of them on the fastest of the two sloops and took his seat under an awning. 'A strong breeze was blowing and the sailors were delighted to please Montezuma. They worked the sails so well, that they went flying along and the canoes which held his huntsmen and the rest of the courtiers were left far behind in spite of the large number of rowers they carried. Montezuma was charmed and said it was a great art this combining of oars and sails.' They were soon at the island and had a successful day's hunting. On getting back Montezuma did not omit to tip the Spaniards. 'He was such a great Prince, so frank and kind,' adds Bernal.

But Montezuma's most dazzling generosity was to come. One day he told Cortés that he had decided to give Charles V the treasure hidden in the sealed room. 'I know you opened the door and saw it,' he said. 'Well, I want it all to go to your great king.'

Though the Spaniards had long resolved to take the treasure, they were greatly touched by the offer to give it. 'Cortés and all of us stood amazed at the vast goodness and liberality of the Great Montezuma. With much reverence we doffed our helmets and returned him thanks. Cortés using words of the greatest affection promised to write to His Majesty of the magnificent generosity of the gift.'

The rule was, as we know, that the Emperor had a right to a fifth of treasure, tribute, revenue or the like received by his representatives in America. Though Montezuma had said all the treasure was to go to him, the Spaniards had no intention of sending it all. At Vera Cruz they had sent all, but there were special reasons on that occasion. For the present, indeed, it was impossible to send any of it, since Cortés had no ship. However, the Royal Fifth was duly put aside. Then the squabble began about the shares. Cortés, as Charles's representative, in legal fiction if not in actual fact, claimed a fifth for himself; he claimed also the share of a Captain-General; and he claimed for expenses, starting with what he had spent in Cuba to equip the expedition and including all expenditure and losses since. The Captains and the three churchmen also put in heavy claims. When all these had been met, only enough remained to give the rank and file the value of a hundred gold pieces each. As the total value of the treasure was supposed to be about a million gold pieces, the soldiers were grievously disappointed. In spite of the presents, most of them were in debt. They had so far received no pay, only promises. They had thought Montezuma's treasure was going to make their fortunes. The way Cortés arranged the share-out looked mean in comparison with Montezuma's noble generosity; and it looked tricky too, says Bernal. We cannot hope to make up accounts which those concerned could not agree on four hundred years ago. But the affair left a bad taste in Bernal's mouth and provides another indication of his partiality for Montezuma. However, in the long run the share-out did not matter because, as we shall see, the treasure was lost.

Though the Spaniards had a tenderness for Montezuma, there was the other side of his character to give them pause, the monstrous side, the religious side, when as priest-king he took life that the gods might live. During these months, November 1519 to April 1520, several important Mexican festivals fell due, the great Humming Bird's on November 22nd, the rain god,

Tlaloc's, on December 12th, Ilamatecutli (The Old Lady's) feast on January 1st, and the fire god's, Xiuhtecutli (The Turquoise Lord), on January 21st. Montezuma, though resident with Cortés, continued to carry out his religious duties as usual. 'From one day to another he never ceased his sacrifices at which human beings were killed,' says Bernal. In his own palace, as we know, he had cages of victims and a private sacrificial stone. It is hardly to be supposed that with the rest of his things he moved these across to Lord Face of Water's palace, as Cortés had forbidden him to make human sacrifices. Nevertheless he seems to have managed. Perhaps he was able to slip into his own palace for a moment, as it was practically next door. That should have been easy, as he was on such good terms with the Spaniards. The fact was that he dared not neglect his religious duties. He was more convinced of the necessity of the magic rituals than was Cortés of the Mass. The Mass insured individual salvation after death; his rituals insured that humanity could live.

Cortés was doing his best to convert him to Christianity. One wonders how the Gospel story came through Doña Marina's mouth. What did Montezuma make of it, what could he make of it? Christianity could only be the religion which Quetzalcoatl had taught in his previous visit to earth. If there was no alternative to receiving Quetzalcoatl, was there any to accepting his religion? This difficult question, which has been hanging over us for some time and whose answer cannot be longer deferred, again illustrates Montezuma's agonizing dilemma. Quetzalcoatl on his last visit had preached against the old gods and their ritual of sacrifice. And what had happened? The old gods had struck back. Smoking Mirror, their leader, had won. Quetzalcoatl had had to go. But that was not all. The gods, much displeased at the attempt to displace them, had punished the ruling race, which, as stated, was at that time the Toltecs. Disasters overtook it; it passed out of existence. This clash with the old gods must be avoided this time, if the

Mexica (People of the Maguey Hare) were to survive. The only
way a clash could be avoided would be by retaining the old
worship while accepting the new. The new religion would have
its temples, but the old temples would be kept up. Montezuma had a basis for this plan. The worship of Quetzalcoatl
already existed at Cholula. His ritual could be brought up-to-
date, more temples built. He could be advanced without undue
detriment to the ancient deities. Instead of the Spaniards chris-
tianizing Mexico, the Mexicans could weave christianity into
their own system of thought.

But Montezuma was painfully aware that to steer such a
course was exceedingly difficult. The gods were already angry
at what had happened. He was far from forgetting the terrible
apparition of Smoking Mirror to his magicians. Any day a
message might be conveyed to him from the Humming Bird
or the others, speaking through priest-mediums at the time of
sacrifice, that Quetzalcoatl was to be driven out. The supernatural clash he so much hoped to avoid would then be inevitable, with incalculably evil results for the nation. His right,
his only, course was to propitiate the old gods with the magic
sacrifices which they demanded, at the same time protecting
Cortés by every means in his power.

Thanks to Bernal, who records such a great deal of what he
saw, though he did not always understand its inner meaning,
there has come down to us a view of Montezuma when he
visited the great temple opposite Lord Face of Water's palace,
probably to attend the rain god, Tlaloc's, festival, whose shrine
was next to the Humming Bird's on top of the pyramid. He
had asked Cortés' permission, as he wished to go in state and
in the most public manner, so as to reassure the people that
he was not neglecting the gods. Cortés gave permission provided there was no sacrifice of human beings.

Montezuma 'set off in his rich litter accompanied by many
of his lords. His staff of office was carried before him. A company of Spaniards followed.' The Padre de la Merced, one of

the churchmen, was with them. They entered the immense courtyard of the temple through the Serpent Wall. The first thing they saw was the *tlachtli* court, where the game was played whose balls, as I have mentioned, were made of rubber exported by the Totonacs. It was not played for amusement, but for magical reasons; was not a sport but a ritual. At the Humming Bird's feast on November 22nd, for instance, a priest dressed as the Messenger of Death descended from the top of the pyramid to the ball court and killed four slave victims in it. To the left of the ball court was the prison where captives awaiting sacrifice were kept. On the right was the small temple of Xipe, a vegetation god, whose magic ritual had the horrid peculiarity that the victims were flayed after their hearts had been taken out, and their skins worn by dancers for twenty days, until they rotted. (It is curious to remark that this ritual inspired some of the greatest Mexican works of art, such as the stone mask in the British Museum, which represents the skin of the face of a sacrificed victim, a work where horror dissolves in beauty, for us a mystery, but not so for the artist, for whom the sacrifice had a magical beauty.)

Making their way inward with Montezuma's procession, the Spaniards next passed a skull rack similar to ones they had already seen, and said to contain over 100,000 skulls. Here to the left was the Calmecatl (House of the Cord), a sort of theological college, and to the right the Temalacatl (Stone Ring), a small circular platform on which victims to be sacrificed to Xipe were tethered by one leg, given a wooden sword edged with down feathers instead of obsidian razors, and made to fight against four fully armed soldiers, a sort of contest which the Romans at their worst included in the gladiatorial games, but which in Mexico was not a cruel sport but part of a magical ritual to make the maize-shoot burst from the seed.

The procession now reached the open space in front of the main pyramid temple, which rose steeply to its summit at the top of a great flight of over a hundred steps. On the platform were the shrines of the Humming Bird and of Tlaloc, the rain god, and before each was a sacrificial stone.

Bernal now tells what happened on this occasion. 'When we first came to the gate of the cursed temple, Montezuma ordered them to take him from his litter and he was carried on the shoulders of lords to the foot of the steps. There many priests were waiting to support him under the arms in the ascent. They had already sacrificed in the night four human victims. In spite of what Cortés had said and now the dissuasions of the Padre de la Merced, he paid no heed, but persisted in killing men and boys to complete the sacrifice. We could no nothing but pretend not to notice it. When he had finished sacrificing, and he did not take long about it, we returned with him to our quarters. He was very cheerful and gave presents of golden jewels to us soldiers who accompanied him.'

Before concluding this chapter two questions require to be answered. Why did Montezuma give so many presents to the Spaniards and what would have happened if Cortés had succeeded in converting him to Christianity? The answers to both help to clarify the complex situation.

Montezuma had several reasons for his presents. The most obvious one was that he hoped thereby to keep the Spaniards in a good humour and avoid further humiliations. If they were in his pay, he had a hold on them. Who exactly they were, however, he did not know. At first, as the companions of Cortés, they had all seemed supernatural beings. Bernal frequently states that they were openly called *teules*, his rendering of the Nauatl word, *teotl*, god. But when Montezuma began to think that Cortés-Quetzalcoatl had not come direct from an eastern paradise, but from a country ruled by a great king, the Spaniards had to be thought of as servants of that king. They were human beings, yet as the assistants of a divine incarnation they had magical powers. It was therefore fitting to make offerings to them. Even the most minor local deities were given offerings.

This conception of the presents as offerings applied, of course, more obviously to those which he gave to Cortés. The gift of the treasure was an oblation. Just as he gave the other gods hearts, which was what they required in their ghostly state, so he gave Cortés-Quetzalcoatl gold, which was what he required as a reincarnated divine ghost. And inasmuch as he gave the unapparent gods all the hearts he had or could get, so he must give the apparent god all the gold he had or could get.

In addition to this grand motive, he had yet a further motive for giving the treasure. It will be recalled that his greatest hope was that Cortés would not stay long. Though at the time of his coming he had declared himself an envoy with a message, who would return whence he came without undue delay, he had since shown no sign of departing. But, argued Montezuma, if I give him all the gold I have, perhaps he will go, for since it is gold he requires, and I am giving him a great quantity, that will suffice him for his purposes, just as the hearts I give the other gods, which are all I have, suffice them for their purposes. Moreover, I will send him gold yearly, as I get it in. If I can induce him to go before the other gods are roused to some furious action, I shall have saved my country. The expenditure of all my gold is not too great a price to pay. So he dared hope though the prophecy hardly allowed a glimmer.

And now let us consider the second question. What would have happened if Cortés had been able to persuade Montezuma to believe in Christianity? Here we find a startling paradox which provides the final proof that Cortés had not grasped the elements of the situation as they were understood by Montezuma. If Montezuma had become a Christian, he would have ceased to believe in Quetzalcoatl. The incursion of Cortés would have been revealed to him in its true light. He would have seen Cortés for what he was, an invader whose intention was to destroy the legitimate government of Mexico and take possession of the country. The duty of Montezuma, as a Christian sovereign, would have been to fight Cortés, drive him out or make him prisoner or kill him. There was nothing in Christianity as interpreted at that date in Europe which gave Cortés or Charles V any excuse for remaining in Mexico if its sovereign was a Catholic. The paradox, then, resides in this— that Cortés was doing his best to dispel the illusion which was his only guarantee of safety. However, he had no chance of dispelling it. Having been fitted into the Mexican astro-magical picture of the universe and, so, satisfactorily explained from their point of view, it was no more possible for him to explain himself otherwise than it would have been for Montezuma to explain that he was other than a man deluded by the Devil.

⟨17⟩

The Installation of the Virgin

Before giving Cortés the treasure, Montezuma allowed him at this time to send Spaniards all over Mexican territory to inspect the gold mines and estimate their output. He also offered to let him have that part of the tribute which was paid in gold by his 371 vassal towns. All seemed going well for Cortés. As this large and regular income began to come in, his position would be greatly strengthened. He would have enough gold to meet all the calls he anticipated in the future. He could pay his troops in the liberal way they expected; recruit more Spaniards from the West Indies; send to Charles V and his advisers a stream of gold which would overcome all opposition in that quarter; and have enough, if necessary, to square his chief, Diego Velázquez, who, though nothing had been heard of him since he had been so neatly squeezed out of the venture, might still be capable of making himself unpleasant. Gold, in fact, was the answer to everything.

But now the tide began to turn. It was very difficult for Cortés to know whether to press the pace or go slow. Though Montezuma had accepted him as ruler of Mexico for a number of strange reasons, some understandable and some not, who could say whether popular opinion would continue indefinitely to acquiesce? Up to date, except for Lord Maize Cobs and his adherents, the people generally had endorsed their sovereign's actions. But the necks of all possible opponents were not in Cortés' chain. A new leader might appear and render Montezuma powerless. If Montezuma lost his power, his own power would evaporate. He would be back where he was at the start—the commander of a few hundred men in the middle of a lake surrounded by armed forces outnumbering him a hundredfold.

The quarter from which he thought opposition was most likely to arise was the Mexican church, the Devil's foundation. The images of the gods, though the work of men's hands, were possessed by devils and there emanated from them an evil power, just as there emanated from an image of the Virgin a good power. On the occasion when, five days after his arrival, Cortés visited the Tlatelolco temple in the north quarter of the city he had said to Montezuma, as Bernal records: 'These idols of yours are not gods, but evil things which are called devils. Do me the favour to approve of my placing a Cross here on the top of this pyramid and in one part of these shrines allow me to set up an image of Our Lady. You will see by the fear in which these idols hold her that they are deceiving you.' Montezuma had refused and now Cortés resolved to press him again. An image of the Virgin, erected in the great temple opposite the Spanish quarters, would give forth a sacred radiance powerful enough to counteract the witchery directed against them by the Devil through the images of himself which he had deceived the Mexicans into making. It should be added here that Cortés, while he was certainly shocked, as we should be shocked, by the spectacle of human sacrifice, was, unlike us, afraid of the sacrifices because they were invocations of the Devil. The Spaniards, besides the reasons supplied by Catholic divines of the period, had a particular reason for believing the Mexican gods were the mouthpieces of the Devil. When the priests fell into trance before the images, as it is known that they did, strange voices, some like the twittering of birds, could be heard, the same sort of voices that come from mediums at séances anywhere. If the Virgin's presence alarmed the Devil and his agents in the images, they would not dare to speak and so the most dangerous inspirer of disaffection would be silenced.

Some historians have argued that Cortés held a more rationalistic view of the gods than this. I do not think so. The magical rituals of the Mexican church seemed to him witchcraft, the deadly science of invoking the Devil.

An image of the Virgin could only be placed in the great temple if Montezuma gave leave, because only he could restrain the resentment of the priests which such an act was bound to arouse. As he had refused leave before, Cortés did not now ask him straight out, but used the trick where you demand more than you want, so that what you do want seems moderate in comparison. Accompanied by a party of his men, he went to see Montezuma and told him that they felt so strongly that a shrine should be cleared of its gods and a Cross and Virgin placed there instead, that, since he had refused permission, they had decided to take the law into their own hands. It might happen that the gods would be thrown down. It would be a pity if there was a fight, for priests would be killed. As Cortés said this, his men put on a truculent air, as they had been coached to do.

Montezuma had been dreading that Cortés might bring up this matter again. His authority over the priests and the people had been strained to the uttermost by what he had already done. It would be very hard to get them to stand any more. But dangerous as popular resentment might be, the indignation of the gods themselves was even more to be feared. His first impulse was to try to gain time. According to Bernal, he said to Cortés: 'Oh, Malintzin! how can you wish to destroy the city completely! Our gods are very angry with us. I do not know that they will stop even at your lives. Please be patient for a little while. I will summon the priests and see what they say.'

Cortés then ordered his party to withdraw and told Montezuma that he wanted a confidential word with him. When they were alone together he said that he could restrain his men, if

The Installation of the Virgin

Montezuma ordered a shrine to be cleared. The Cross and the Virgin could then quietly be installed without danger of the gods being mishandled or the priests molested. Montezuma was still very distressed, but declared he would try to persuade the priests. He sent for them and after much discussion he got them to agree to let the Spaniards use a shrine as a Christian chapel.

What happened after that is not quite clear. In a letter to Charles V Cortés boasts that he overturned some statues or other from their pedestals and rolled them down the steps of the pyramid. But throughout his letters to His Most Christian Majesty he assumes the poses that he thought his master would like. Bernal says nothing about this outrage. The other eye-witness, Andrés de Tapia, however, declares he saw Cortés hit a god with a crowbar and knock off his golden mask. I think we must take it that the Spaniards, impatient perhaps because the priests were slow at clearing the promised shrine, lost their tempers and began knocking the images about. There was a moment when it was touch and go whether the priests would attack them. It seems, however, that Cortés was able to restore calm. The shrine was cleaned of blood, the Cross and Virgin were installed and Mass said with all propriety.

ᴄɪ8ᴈ

The Smoking Mirror Demands Cortés' Death

It would be reasonable to suppose that Cortés, on reflection, felt qualms at the imprudence of his behaviour at the temple. It had been much more offensive than he had originally intended. He had incensed the priesthood, and thereby weakened Montezuma's authority, the maintenance of which was a prime necessity. But he does not seem to have realized that he had gone too far. It was as though he were satisfied that the Cross and the Virgin, now standing over against the Devil's impersonations, would confound them and render impotent their ministers.

If this was his anticipation, he had miscalculated. Bernal writes that shortly afterwards the priests reported to Montezuma that the Smoking Mirror had ordered all the Spaniards to be killed. If their order were not obeyed, they would forsake the city.

On getting this message, which presumably came from the Chief Priest, the second member of the Council, who had so far supported him, Montezuma was brought face to face with his dilemma. If he disobeyed the gods and they abandoned Mexico, the cosmic order, which it was the sole object of the religion to maintain, would be disrupted. Without the Humming Bird, the god of war, victims could not be procured. If Tlaloc absented himself, it would not rain. If Xipe departed, the maize would not sprout. If Tonatiuh went elsewhere, the sun would not rise. Such a general strike of the forces of nature would be the end of Mexico, the end of the world. On the other hand, for him to give the order for his army to destroy Quetzalcoatl along with his followers would be to commit sacrilege against the Eastern Quarter of the sky, against the Morning Star, the harbinger of dawn, and against the Wind, who swept the road for the rain clouds. That the gods might lay this duty upon him or in default themselves destroy Quetzalcoatl, thereafter punishing him and his people for disobedience, had been the terror haunting him from the beginning.

But now it occurred to him that the middle course which he had kept throughout might still avert complete disaster. The situation, discreetly handled, might even turn to his advantage. If he used it to achieve what he had always striven for, though latterly with diminishing hope, namely Quetzalcoatl's departure, the gods would waive their order to kill him and the crisis would be over.

He sent an urgent message to Cortés asking him to call. There may have been rumours of unrest in the city, for Cortés, on receiving the summons, hastened over to the royal apartments. Montezuma came to the point at once. 'I am deeply distressed to have to inform you,' he said, 'that the gods have ordered me to make war on you. On thinking it over I have come to the conclusion that the best course for you all is to leave the city at once before the attack begins. It is a question of your lives. Nothing else can save them.'

On hearing these words, says Bernal, 'Cortés was a good deal disquieted. And that was not to be wondered at. The warning had come so suddenly and had been uttered with such insistence on our danger.' But it was not Cortés' nature to be upset for

long, and he collected himself in a moment. The greater the
danger, the cooler he always grew, and the more resourceful and
the craftier. He began his reply by thanking Montezuma sin-
cerely for the warning and advice. Then, his voice changing, he
said he would gladly take the advice and go, were he not
troubled by two difficulties. 'For one thing,' he said, 'I have no
ships to sail away in; for another, you would have to come with
us, for our Emperor would want to see you.' This last, no
doubt, was a bit of bluff, which, if it frightened Montezuma,
would make him more amenable. It did frighten him. He
apparently accepted it as a mandate which he would have to
obey, and was very cast down, though he could not have been
carried away against his will. Was it, as before, that he dared
not disobey the god except in those cases where disobedience
would have embroiled him fatally with the other gods? Or was
it that in crediting Cortés with godhead, he credited him also
with a reserve of magical power, which in certain conjunctions
of time, place and direction would have the force of an enchantment? The magical system of the Mexicans was very intricate,
far more so than would suggest the simplifications which for
clarity's sake I have been obliged to employ. Every moment of
their lives was governed by its rules. Montezuma may have
worked out the magical equation which represented his relation
to Cortés and have deduced conclusions from it that applied to
this occasion. That there should be such difficulty in explaining
so comparatively minor a point shows how little we can penetrate into the maze of his thoughts.

Though Cortés had scored a point and saved his face, the
danger was very real. He went on to say that though for want of
ships he could not go at once, he would send orders to the
garrison at Vera Cruz to have three ships built. Montezuma
was relieved to hear this and said he would supply carpenters to
help the shipwrights. 'They shall be instructed,' he said, 'to
hurry and not waste time in talk. Meanwhile I will command
the priests and military not to stir up disturbances in the city

and direct that the gods be appeased with sacrifices.' And added: 'Though not of human beings.'

That Cortés intended to leave when the ships were ready need not be assumed. Their building was both a precaution and a way of gaining time.

The Spaniards now passed through an anxious week or so. Bernal writes: 'We all went about in low spirits, fearing that at any moment they might attack us. Our friends from Tlaxcala and Doña Marina also told the Captain that an attack was probable, and Orteguilla, Montezuma's page, was always in tears. Neither by day nor night did we ever take off our arms or gorgets or leggings, and we slept in them. Maybe some will ask what the beds were like. They were nothing but a little straw and a mat.'

The thought of these exciting days sets him talking of himself, a thing he rarely does, which is a pity, for he was a delightful character. 'I want to say, though not with the intention of boasting about it, that I grew so accustomed to sleeping fully dressed and on a mat, that after the conquest I kept to the habit and I slept better thus than if properly in bed. There is another thing, too, I must mention. I am only able to sleep for a short time of a night, and have to get up and look at the heavens and the stars, and walk about for a time in the dew. This I do without putting a cap or handkerchief on my head. I am so used to it that, thank God, it does me no harm. But I must stop talking like this, for I am wandering from my story.'

${19}$

Velázquez's Counterstroke is Defeated

It was at this moment of crisis in Mexico that Velázquez made his counter-stroke.

It will be recalled that in July 1519 Cortés sent his envoy Puertocarrero to deliver to Charles V the golden wheel and other presents and the letters which told what had happened up to that date. With Puertocarrero was another envoy, Francisco de Montejo. They had strict orders to sail to Spain without touching at Cuba, as it was essential that Velázquez should not learn about the founding of Vera Cruz and how he had been ousted from the venture. But the order to avoid Cuba was disobeyed. Both envoys landed there at an out of the way spot on August 23rd. Details of Cortés' success in Mexico leaked out, and an informer hastened across the island to tell Velázquez the news. He immediately sent men to seize the envoys, but they escaped and reached Spain safely in October 1519. They were anticipated, however, by letters denouncing Cortés as a traitor, which Velázquez managed to get by a fast sailer to his influential friends at the Court of Spain. In result, Puertocarrero and Montejo had obstacles put in their way and it was not until April 1520 that they could see Charles and give him the presents. But, though they had audience again in May, they failed to get him to recognize Cortés as his representative in Mexico. He could not make up his mind on the case. Neither Cortés' nor Velázquez's position was defined. The matter was left open and no pronouncement made until 1522. Only in the October of that year did Cortés receive official recognition.

But Velázquez, believing his friends at Court would win the case for him, resolved to be avenged at once. During the winter of 1519-20, when Cortés' envoys were striving to get Charles' ear, he began to assemble ships and men to send to Mexico, take over the country in his name and arrest Cortés, whom he intended to hang. By strenuous efforts and a large expenditure of money he collected an armada of some twenty vessels, carrying 1,300 men, a park of 10 field guns, 80 horses, 80 musketeers and 120 crossbowmen. This force, many times greater than Cortés', left Cuba in March 1520 and arrived on the Mexican coast at San Juan de Ulúa in the middle of April. It was commanded by a Spanish resident of Cuba named Pamfilo de Narváez. Though he carried Velázquez's written orders to proceed against Cortés by force, Narváez had, not only no authorization from Charles, but also none from the Viceregal government of Hispaniola, to which Cuba was subordinate. Indeed, the Viceregal government had first expressly forbidden Velázquez to send the fleet, and when he insisted on doing so, allowed it to go only on condition that he negotiated a settlement with his rival; for it was deemed highly undesirable that fighting should occur between Spaniards in the New World. A Viceregal representative named Ayllón was sent with the fleet to keep an eye on Narváez. On reaching San Juan de Ulúa, however, Narváez managed to disembarrass himself of Ayllón and sent him back to Hispaniola.

Cortés in his letter to the Emperor describing his encounter with Narváez says that the first news was a messenger's report that one ship had been sighted. He hoped this was Puerto-acrrero returning with the Emperor's recognition and perhaps with reinforcements, for he was due back about this time. More messengers, however, arrived and he learnt the true facts. A huge force had been sent against him; the eighty horses were an especially alarming feature. He had been taken entirely by surprise, and at a moment, too, when his troops were not at full strength, for he had sent a contingent of 150 men under a captain de León to explore in one direction and 110 men under a captain de Rangel to explore in another. But he had a winning card with his gold. He calculated that he had enough gold to debauch the whole of Narváez's army. Later, when he discovered that Narváez had no authority from the Emperor, he used his own sounder legal position with effect. He had another advantage, too. Though his troops were so inferior in numbers, they were veterans, while Narváez's men had been living a soft life on the Cuban plantations. Without undue conceit he knew himself to be the better commander. He was far the more experienced, had won extraordinary victories, knew the country and had supporters there. All in all, Narváez would be child's play after the perils of the past. The fellow could be undermined with guile and gold, and then smashed with a blow that would teach Velázquez not to meddle again.

But there was Montezuma. How would it go there? The mysterious king was his prisoner; he was the prisoner of the mysterious king. Dealing with a Narváez was plain sailing in comparison with solving the puzzle of Montezuma's intentions. With Narváez you spoke the language of your period; with Montezuma words lost their meaning, all was topsy-turvy, you were god, man, star, wind, all at the same time. How would he take the coming of Narváez? You could not tell. It was past imagination. Well, he would go and have a talk with him.

Montezuma, who still was carrying on the day-to-day administration of his country, had received the news as soon as Cortés. His agents on the coast sent him post-haste a detailed report in the picture writing. But he could not make head or tail of it.

Who could Narváez be? A rival god or what? An adjutant of Cortés or an envoy from Charles? If another god, he should be propitiated. If an adjutant, then perhaps Cortés intended to leave with him. Could it be that the end of his troubles was in sight? In any event he should encourage Narváez to stay. Word was sent to the people on the coast to give him food and presents. (Montezuma may also have dallied with the idea that Narváez, if an opponent of Cortés, might overcome him and so assume responsibility for what Montezuma himself dared not be responsible. But if he held such an idea, he soon seems to have dismissed it.)

Bernal records two conversations between Cortés and Montezuma at this time. At the first of them he puts words in Montezuma's mouth which are consistent with my last paragraph. Montezuma says: 'Now you will have no need to build ships. I was delighted at the arrival of your brothers, for now you can all return home.'

Cortés did not give him on this occasion any explanation of Narváez's coming. In the second conversation Montezuma says: 'I do not understand it at all,' and asks whether it is true that Cortés intends to march against Narváez, as he had heard the page Orteguilla declare. Cortés replied it was true, and now explained that Narváez, though he had come from the dominions of the great Emperor, was a bandit whom it was his duty to arrest. 'Though he has large forces and we are few, Our Lady will give us strength to overcome him,' he said.

Montezuma accepted this explanation. As his belief in Cortés' identity was unshaken, he thought it unlikely that Narváez would be able to prevail. 'I can let you have five thousand soldiers if you like,' he said. Cortés thanked him, but replied impressively that the help of God and his companions would suffice. And he went on that he would leave eighty soldiers under Alvarado in Lord Face of Water's palace. He hoped Montezuma would remain there as before, and see to it that Alvarado had enough to eat. 'You need not be anxious,' he assured him. 'We shall soon be back victorious. Stay quietly with Alvarado and keep the priests from making a row.' Saying so he embraced Montezuma twice, and Montezuma embraced him in return.

We cannot hope to penetrate Montezuma's thoughts altogether. He had hoped that Cortés would go for good, and now heard he was coming back. He had warned him a little time before that an attack would be made on him at the instigation of the gods, if he did not go. To bring these facts into line, we must suppose he believed that Cortés, after defeating Narváez and capturing his ships, would depart on them or could be induced to depart on them. This was not an unreasonable belief, for it remained incontrovertible that if the Mexicans rose against him he could not maintain himself in Mexico.

Before Cortés marched on Narváez, he turned Lord Face of Water's palace into a fortress and provisioned it. He warned Alvarado to be careful, and added to the force of 80 Spaniards he was leaving some 400 Tlaxcalans who had volunteered to stay. The garrison was to look after Montezuma, guard the treasure and hold out till he returned. His own force numbered only 70 men. But when, as he hoped, he had joined up with de León and de Rangel, who had been ordered to meet him *en route*, he would have 330 men, good enough when his gold had prepared the way.

Bernal has some amusing anecdotes how this was done. The appetite of Narváez's men was whetted early on by three renegades who left Cortés' employ on the coast and went aboard the ships. One of them, who happened to be a professional jester, said laughing: 'How fortunate you are, Narváez, to have come at this time when that traitor of a Cortés has got together treasure worth more than 700,000 gold pieces!' On their inquiring whether this was one of his jokes, he became serious and gave them the details.

Sandoval had taken over the command at Vera Cruz after Escalante's death. When Narváez learned of the town's whereabouts, he did not march immediately and take it, though Sandoval had only forty men fit to fight, but despatched envoys to demand its surrender. Sandoval arrested them and ordered them to be sent to Mexico, as Cortés had not yet started. Totonac porters, working in relays, carried them there in hammocks. They were on the way four nights and days without stopping and arrived frightened and bewildered, half-inclined, says Bernal, to believe it was all witchcraft or a dream. But Cortés, warned of their coming, had them met outside the city, provided horses for the last lap, and when they appeared before him apologized for the treatment they had received. He entertained them for two days, took them sightseeing, let them have a glimpse of the treasure, gave them some gold and made them promises of more. 'Although they had set out fierce as lions, they returned thoroughly tamed,' says Bernal. 'Cortés sent them back with food for the road. After reporting to Narváez, they began to persuade all the camp to come over to our side.'

Cortés followed this up by writing a very friendly letter to Narváez, offering to place himself entirely at his disposal and suggesting an amicable division of the country. Why fight, he asked, and reduce both our forces? The whole country will rise if they see us divided. He hoped this would put Narváez off his guard. The letter was entrusted to the Padre de la Merced. The Padre also carried letters addressed to other captains and a quantity of gold to distribute as presents. On his arrival at the coast, he went to kiss Narváez's hands and repeated Cortés' offer of friendship. 'But Narváez who was very obstinate would not listen to him and used abusive language. Then the Padre very secretly distributed the ingots and chains of gold he had with him to those named by Cortés, and so won over the chief persons in Narváez's camp.' But there was a captain called Salvatierra who 'swore he would roast Cortés' ears and eat one of them'. That was only his talk, however, for he was a cowardly fellow.

By these devices Cortés had half-conquered Narváez before

he and his seventy men started for the coast in the first week of May 1520. 'Without taking any women or any servants with us, and marching in light order, we set out for Cholula,' the town on the other side of the volcanoes which they had occupied on their way in. From there Cortés wrote to the lords of Tlaxcala, asking for a contingent of 6,000 men, but the Tlaxcalans excused themselves, saying they were ready any day to fight the Mexicans, but that the prospect of facing fire-arms, horsemen and crossbowmen did not appeal to them. To prove their goodwill, however, they sent twenty loads of turkey, about a thousand pounds' weight.

The route taken after Cholula was not the same as on the inward march. It was shorter, straight across via the volcano of Orizaba. Montezuma had provided men to guide them. On the way they met a notary whom Narváez had sent to serve a demand for Cortés' surrender. Cortés politely dismounted and asked his business. The notary explained. When Cortés desired him to produce his credentials from the Emperor Charles, he was taken aback. His only credentials were from Velázquez. Seeing him confused, Cortés cheered him up, gave him a present of gold and sent him back to Narváez. The man, says Bernal, did not fail to spread the news that Cortés was an open-handed gentleman.

By this time Cortés had been joined by the contingents of de León and de Rangel and his army numbered 330. As he approached the coast Sandoval came up with his forty men. From them he learnt the latest news. Narváez had been making himself very unpleasant. Sandoval had been obliged to evacuate Vera Cruz and take refuge among the Totonacs of the hills. The fat lord of Cempoalan had had a dreadful time. Narváez had taken from him the gold and mantles which Cortés had sent him as presents. He also seized the girls who had been given to Cortés' captains, some of whom, at least, had been left behind at Cempoalan, as they were ladies and unaccustomed to long walks. When the fat lord complained that Cortés would kill him if he found the girls missing, Narváez made fun of him, and Salvatierra said: 'Considering that Cortés is a mere nobody, it is amusing to see what a fright this fellow is in.' However, said Sandoval, Salvatierra was neatly paid back. Two soldiers disguised as Totonacs went to Narváez's camp with plums to sell. They hung about and after dark stole Salvatierra's horse. The story made Cortés laugh. 'Salvatierra will have to do a lot more boasting to make up for that,' he said.

Cortés now moved closer in to Cempoalan where Narváez was encamped. He asked a Totonac town to let him have two thousand soldiers. He also had a quantity of long pikes made locally for his men to use against the eighty horsemen on the other side. While engaged in these and other preparations for the battle which was drawing near, he continued to make a show of negotiating with Narváez, and even sent de León to pretend that he might be induced to betray Cortés.

Some days passed thus. Then without waiting for the Totonac contingent, Cortés advanced to a river three miles south of Cempoalan, and halted with the river covering his front. Narváez, believing that at last an attack was coming, drew up his force north of the river. But as no attack materialized that day, and since it was raining heavily and his men complained, he withdrew again into the comfort of Cempoalan, posting scouts to give him information immediately if Cortés crossed the river.

When Cortés heard this, he decided on a surprise attack that very night. He drew up his small force and made them a splendid oration. As he knew well how to talk to soldiers, he soon had them in fighting mood, though they were soaked to the skin and had had no supper. The orders were: a captain called Pizarro was to seize the artillery; and Sandoval with sixty companions was to single out Narváez and capture him. A reward of three thousand gold pieces was promised to the man who first laid hands on him. A price was also put on Salvatierra. Cortés wound up: 'I know well that the followers of

Velázquez's Counterstroke is Defeated

Narváez are four times as numerous as we are, but they are not used to arms, and as the greater part of them are disaffected towards him and we shall take them by surprise, I have an idea that God will give us the victory.' The password was 'The Holy Ghost', as it was the eve of Pentecost. Bernal adds: 'When all this was finished, as I was a great friend of Captain Sandoval, he begged me as a favour to keep by him that night and follow him if I were still alive after capturing the artillery.'

Like all Cortés' important battles, the battle ahead was a case of victory or complete ruin. Still unrecognized by Charles, declared a traitor by Velázquez, with the Totonac federation sitting on the fence, his allies the Tlaxcalans unwilling to send a man, and the Mexicans in his rear divinely inspired to make an end of him, he had no one to turn to. But he found in himself all the assurance he required.

In the small hours of the morning (it was May 29th) he gave the order to advance. The drums beat, the men formed up. Heavy rain was still falling. They waded into the river, which though swollen, was just fordable. 'I remember', says Bernal, 'that the stones were slippery and that as the water was deep we were much encumbered with our pikes and other arms.' On the farther bank they presently came upon two scouts posted there by Narváez to give him warning. One of them they seized, but the other ran back to give the alarm. They could hear him crying in panic: 'To arms, to arms, Cortés is coming!' This spoiled a complete surprise, but by following as fast as possible they reached Cempoalan not very far behind him.

Cempoalan had some fortifications, but Narváez, whose intention was to fight outside on the plain, where he would have room to deploy his superior numbers, had not bothered to man them, as he had dismissed the possibility of a night attack. His force was encamped in a temple enclosure. Like those in Mexico city, this was a large courtyard containing several steep pyramids. He had perched his troops on their platforms. His head-quarters were on the biggest platform, on the lower steps of which he had mounted his guns. The effect of this arrangement was to split up his force, an error that was to prove fatal. His horsemen were on ground level, but could be of little use with the darkness and lack of space.

Cortés learnt some of these details from the scout he had taken prisoner, and, as he knew Cempoalan well, had no difficulty in finding the way to the temple courtyard. Narváez, who had had to be woken up, was in the act of rallying his men. Without a moment's hesitation, Pizarro made for the guns. The gunners had only time to fire two or three pieces before they were overpowered. Sandoval then led his sixty men up the pyramid steps to capture Narváez, while Cortés remained at the bottom to direct operations and repulse those who might come to Narváez's assistance. Bernal says that, as he had promised, he followed Sandoval up the pyramid. 'We stood for some time fighting with our long pikes and when I was least expecting it we heard Narváez cry out: "Holy Mary protect me! They have killed me and destroyed my eye." At this, we shouted: "Victory for the Holy Spirit, victory for Cortés! Narváez has fallen, Narváez is dead!" ' Fire was set to the thatched roof of the shrines on the platform and the defenders came tumbling down the steps. Among them was Narváez, who was immediately secured. One of his eyes had been put out by a pike thrust.

It remained to deal with the men on the other platforms in the courtyard. Had they come down and made a concerted onslaught on Cortés' small force they might have prevailed. But no one gave them the order. One detects here the influence of the gold. The captured guns were turned round and fired on them. And when a proclamation was read, calling upon them 'to yield themselves up under the banner of His Majesty, and to Cortés in his Royal name, under pain of death', they began to surrender, shaken in the belief, which they had held till then, that Narváez had written sanction from the Emperor Charles.

Bernal gives us a glimpse of Cortés at about this moment. 'He came without being recognized to where we held Narváez. As the heat was great and he was burdened with his armour, and had been going hither and thither, shouting to our soldiers and making proclamations, he arrived sweating, tired and panting for breath. He had two tries before he could get out what he wanted to ask: "What about Narváez, what about Narváez?" Sandoval cried: "Here he is, here! And well guarded." Said Cortés, still winded: "Take care of him, my son; keep a good hold on him, while I go and make sure his captains have yielded." And he hastened off to issue the proclamation again.' The moon was now sailing free, as the rain had stopped. Fireflies had come out and their light, it was said, mistaken by the followers of Narváez for the match-lights of a large force of musketeers, was a further inducement for them to surrender. As for the cavalry, half of it was captured in the courtyard and the other half, which had galloped out of the town, was induced to return and give itself up.

When all was over and Narváez was having his eye attended to by a surgeon, Cortés came up and, unseen, watched him from the side. Told he was there, Narváez, who was essentially a stupid man, made the fatuous remark: 'Captain Cortés, it has been a great feat, your victory and capture of me.' In a cutting reply Cortés put him in his place: 'I regard it as one of the least important things I have ever done in New Spain.'

Dawn came at last. Cortés, seated in an arm-chair with an orange gown over his armour, received the submission of Narváez's captains. One by one they came up and kissed his hand. He spoke graciously to each, whether the captive of his gold or of his arms, and embraced him in high spirits. 'How cheerful he was!' exclaims Bernal, 'and he had good cause to be, seeing what a great and powerful lord he had become.' He had won a decisive victory between midnight and sunrise and a load was lifted from his mind. He found it amusing also to reflect that his opponents, now mostly ready to take service under him, and to be the reinforcement he badly needed, had been provided at his arch-enemy, Velázquez's, expense.

Bernal fills in the last details. The fat lord, who seems to have completely lost his head when he heard that Cortés was about to enter the city, left his house and took refuge on the pyramid where Narváez was stationed. His conscience must have been very bad. In the mêlée on the pyramid he was wounded. Cortés, who had a soft spot for him, 'ordered him to be well attended and placed in his house so that he should not be molested'. Salvatierra, who was going to fry Cortés' ears, did not live up to the fierce reputation he had given himself. At the first assault he complained of a violent stomach-ache and took no further part in the fighting.

Narváez and Salvatierra were the only two in the expedition whom Cortés ordered to be kept in custody. All the rest, on their volunteering to serve him, he enlisted into his army. He was also careful to seize all the ships. Not one of them was able to slip away to Cuba and carry the disastrous news to Velázquez.

ε20ɜ

The Mexicans Rise against Cortés

Cortés had by this time been absent from Mexico city nearly a month. One of the two dangers that threatened to destroy him had passed away. The other, the gods' mandate that he must leave the country or take the consequences, remained. But the victory over Narváez had greatly improved his situation. According to Bernal, he could now dispose of a combined total of 1,300 men-at-arms, 96 horses, eighty musketeers, as many crossbowmen, and 20 or more pieces of cannon. If he had accomplished so much with some 400 men, surely with such increased numbers he was strong enough to overcome the Mexican priests' opposition. It had been a risk leaving Alvarado with only 80 men, but events had justified it. Convinced that all was well, he even planned before returning to the capital to send part of his troops up the coast to form a settlement and another contingent down it for a similar purpose.

Then suddenly the news arrived from the capital that the Mexicans had risen. The two Tlaxcalan messengers who brought it said that Alvarado was besieged, that fire had been set to his quarters, seven of his men killed and many others wounded, and that help was urgently needed. A letter from Alvarado himself followed to the same effect. Cortés, cancelling his plans for settlements on the coast, resolved to march at once with his whole army to the garrison's relief. Before he started, four lords sent by Montezuma appeared. They explained what had happened. In the middle of May the great festival of Smoking Mirror was held. One of the rituals connected with it was a magical dance held in the courtyard of the temple opposite the Spanish quarters. The dancers were the Mexican nobility, many of whom were of Toltec descent. For the occasion they wore their richest mantles and jewellery. They carried no arms. Alvarado, said the four lords, though he had been consulted about the festival and had raised no objection, sallied out at the head of his armed followers and attacked the dancers, killing as many of them as he could. The city rushed to arms. Alvarado fled back to his quarters, pursued by a mob which tried to storm the place. Montezuma (who of course was inside the building) spoke to the assailants from the wall and managed to calm them. The attacks petered out, but the Mexicans confined the Spaniards, none of whom were allowed to set foot in the city. The envoys concluded by repeating that Alvarado, by his unprovoked attack on a religious occasion, was entirely to blame for the present situation. On hearing their complaint, Cortés, says Bernal, 'was somewhat disgusted and told the messengers that he was going to Mexico and would put all to rights'. His disgust was understandable. Alvarado, always inclined to be rash, had by embittering the Mexicans at this delicate moment greatly increased the power of the opposition which had already demanded that the Spaniards should leave. We should think of these men, not as patriots in any modern sense, but as Smoking Mirror's adherents. It was not that they had begun to doubt that Cortés was Quetzalcoatl. On the contrary, his mishandling of the images of the rival gods and his lieutenant's massacre of the lords in a ritual dance made the identity yet more certain. Where they differed from Montezuma was in the belief that Smoking Mirror could win. Montezuma was convinced that he could not.

The Mexicans Rise against Cortés

The Spanish army left Cempoalan on June 10th and by forced marches reached Tlaxcala in a week, half the time taken to cover the distance on the first march inland. There Cortés learned that though Alvarado had not been attacked again, he remained invested and was short of food. A Tlaxcalan contingent joined the Spaniards and they hastened on. Instead of the Cholula road, the shorter route was taken across country to Tetzcuco, the lake city. On arrival, Cortés received a message from Montezuma, praying him not to be vexed and declaring that what had happened was not done by his wish or consent. Cortés sent a reply that he was not angry in any way, as Montezuma's goodwill was well known to him.

There were disquieting signs, however, that the country had grown disaffected. For instance, none of the lords of Tetzcuco called to pay their respects. Cortés wondered whether, in spite of Montezuma's conciliatory message, his re-entry into the city would be resisted. One of the Spaniards of the garrison rowed across the lake from Mexico to Tetzcuco and reported that his companions were still prevented from leaving their quarters, but were now being sold food. On the whole Cortés inclined to think that he would not be resisted. Elated by his victory over Narváez and the increased size of his army, he came to the conclusion that the Mexicans were afraid of him. But he had never entirely grasped how he stood in Mexico. The Mexicans had never been afraid of him in a physical sense. They had submitted to him for quite different reasons. When he marched on Narváez, he had been able to estimate his chances correctly. But now he was marching towards what was much more difficult to get into perspective.

The sloops had been destroyed during the disturbances. Though Mexico was visible fifteen miles away across the lake, there was no means of getting there except by using one of the three causeways. Their entrances were all at a distance from Tetzcuco, the least far being the one starting from Iztapalapan. But this causeway was about seven miles along, and Cortés,

The Mexicans Rise against Cortés

remembering how very helpless he had felt when crossing by it on his first entry, decided to use the Tacuba causeway, which was only two miles long. Tacuba was right on the opposite side of the lake. They reached it by marching round the north shore. On arrival they found the causeway open and unguarded. They crossed and entered the city. It was June 24th, about noon. No lords came to meet them. Indeed, few people were about. The houses on the main road to the central square seemed deserted. The silence was a little uncanny. However, they reached Lord Face of Water's palace without incident. At their entry, says Bernal, 'the great Montezuma came out to the courtyard to embrace and speak to Cortés, bid him welcome and congratulate him on his victory over Narváez. But Cortés, with the vanity of a conqueror, rebuffed him and Montezuma returned to his apartments with an air of dejection.'

Bernal had already noticed what a great and powerful lord Cortés was delighted to have become after defeating Narváez. Here he lets us see that the Captain-General's conceit of himself had increased till it was less pleasant and more dangerous. Cortés had walked into a trap. Within five days the man to whom he owed his immunity hitherto was to die, and within a week two-thirds of his soldiers were to fall in battle, or perish on the sacrificial stones and be eaten.

⧽21⧼

The Death of Montezuma

As soon as his men were settled in their quarters, Cortés began to question Alvarado about his slaughter of the dancers. The captain's excuse was that he had received information of an attack which was to be made on the Spaniards at the end of the festival. He had thought it prudent to strike first. 'It was very ill done and a great mistake,' Cortés replied angrily, unconvinced that an attack had been meditated. The question was also put whether Montezuma had had a hand in the affair. The soldiers of the garrison who were listening anwered emphatically: 'If Montezuma had had a hand in it, all of us would have perished. On the contrary, he calmed his people till they stopped attacking us.'

The inquiry revealed that Alvarado, thinking to prevent, had precipitated a conflict. How much harm he had done it was hard to say. As far as Cortés could tell, the Mexicans who had attacked did not necessarily belong to the priesthood group which had conveyed the warning of the gods, but probably were connected with it. Whoever precisely they were, their strength was, apparently, not enough to enable them to disobey Montezuma. He still seemed to be recognized as the effective sovereign of the country; nevertheless, though he had saved the garrison, he had already made it plain that the Spaniards would have to go when they had ships to go in; they now had ships and would therefore presumably be asked to go.

Such were the general conclusions warranted by the information available to Cortés on June 24th. But he did not know what had been happening behind the scenes. The opposition to Montezuma had in fact reached a degree of strength which enabled it to disobey. Cortés had re-entered Mexico at the very moment when it was ready to strike. I have said he walked into a trap. He was let into the city because it would be easier to capture the Spaniards inside. But six months' immunity and a new army made him less sensible of the risk of entering what had always been potentially a trap.

Bernal gives some details about Cortés' behaviour on the afternoon and evening of his arrival. Though he had noticed signs of something brewing, he was not perturbed. He saw himself as strong enough to resist Montezuma's request to go, should it again be made. If his tiny garrison of eighty men had been able to beat off attacks (admittedly with Montezuma's help), his force of over a thousand could weather anything. The defeat of Narváez had solved his last problem. He would be able to stay whether Montezuma helped him or not, for he could now maintain himself by his own force. This over-confidence was reflected in his manner to Montezuma. We have seen how rude to him he was at the time of the entry. In the course of the afternoon he was rude to him again. Montezuma sent a message by his lords to say he would like to have a talk with him. Cortés was in an irritable mood. His entry had not been the triumphal progress he had told his new lot of captains to expect—respectful deputations to meet them, presents of gold and mantles, as had happened on the first occasion. There had not been even much of a dinner. They had remarked on this and he felt he had lost face. So now, to show the captains how he could bully Montezuma, he said roughly to the messengers: 'What's the good of a dog who won't keep the markets open and see we are properly fed!' Bernal, who as we know was fond of and admired Montezuma, thought this was disgraceful, as did de León and some of the captains who had remained in Mexico. The latter said: 'Sir, please reflect that if Montezuma had not been so good to us, we should all be dead now and they would have eaten us.' This made Cortés very angry. Bernal says: 'He had so many Spaniards there with him in Mexico that he was in a devil-may-care mood and most discourteously told the messengers to say to Montezuma that if he did not at once order a free flow of market produce it would be the worse for him.'

The point here is that he believed Montezuma's influence over his subjects to be unimpaired, a belief which was sound as far as his information went. But with the rising power of the opposition Montezuma's influence had declined. The opposition now controlled the markets and was making it difficult to get provisions. The garrison had been obliged to buy from private sellers, who charged a high price and could not supply enough. It seems that this came out in a conversation between Cortés and Montezuma later in the afternoon, for, despite the rude message, the two met. In the course of their talk, Montezuma, it appears, suggested that the difficulty over the food could best be overcome, if his brother Cuitlahuac, the lord of Iztapalapan, who with Lord Maize Cobs and other rulers of lake cities had been attached to the chain, were released and sent out to make arrangements. Cortés agreed. Cuitlahuac was released and left the palace. He went straight to the leaders of the opposition. Their head, it now transpired, was a very important man called Quauhtemoctzin (Lord Falling Eagle), Montezuma's first cousin and son of his predecessor, Lord Water Opossum. He held the appointment of Lord of Tlatelolco, the northern half of the city, where the great market was situated. He and his adherents were delighted to see Cuitlahuac, who was the senior lord after Montezuma. A council of state was held and decision taken to appoint him acting sovereign pending the accomplishment of the opposition's design, now openly declared to be the immediate destruction of the Spaniards. Montezuma, thus deprived of his legal powers and the magical authority which was closely interwoven with them, ceased from that instant to have any influence. The theological interpretation, which he had put on the Spanish invasion and which had guided his every action, did not bind the new government.

Some readers may perhaps press me here to be more precise. Is it to be understood that the Council of State, which hitherto had concurred in Montezuma's cosmic interpretation of the Cortés-Quetzalcoatl apparition and in the minutiae of the magical deductions to be drawn therefrom, and so had sanctioned the extraordinary actions their sovereign had felt bound to take, involving surrender of the country, had by some overriding calculation found that his conclusions were wrong? I have suggested before that, in view of the extreme intricacy of Mexican science, the degree of expertness required to draw a conclusion of such importance, and the amount of thought which had been given to the problem over a long period, it was unlikely that the equations, if one may so term them, could have been shown to be fundamentally unsound. Cortés remained the divine incarnation foretold by prophecy. Where the opposition differed from Montezuma was in the action to be taken. Quetzalcoatl in his former incarnation had had to be driven out because the other gods had so decreed. Had he on this occasion been willing to withdraw, as Montezuma always hoped, no opposition party would have gone to extremes. But since he was unwilling to withdraw and the gods again had decreed his expulsion, he must again be hounded from the country or even put to death, whatever the cosmic perils involved. I believe therefore that we should think of the opposition, not as having repudiated Montezuma's interpretation but as having decided to risk a different solution. Their solution did not, moreover, differ so very profoundly from his. His aim had always been to get Cortés to go and latterly he had told him that he must go, as the Mexicans had divine authority for asking this of him and the necessary force to oblige him to obey. The difference lay only in the fact that Montezuma believed that an armed conflict would result in ruin, the magical connotations being what they were, while the opposition believed that it would result in salvation. As we shall see, Montezuma turned out to be right. Resisting Cortés by force led to ruin. But in the meantime Cortés was to suffer a great fall.

With the election of Cuitlahuac, which must have taken place on this same night of June 24th, it was resolved to strike next day. The arms, the men, the plans, were ready. As Cortés was still in ignorance of what was afoot, to delay would be to risk losing the advantage of surprise. To understand the true nature of the insurrection we should be careful, as I have said, not to think of it as a national uprising, but as a variation in the magico-theological conflict which had started as soon as Cortés first landed in the country.

Early the next morning, the 25th, a Spanish soldier was sent along the causeway into Tacuba to fetch some women of Cortés' household, one of them a natural daughter of Montezuma who previously had been given to Cortés as an additional consort. During his absence they had been staying with the lord of Tacuba. As the soldier made his way back with them he found the causeway blocked by Mexican soldiers. They took the women from him and wounded him. He managed to escape and ran to the Spanish quarters. In a panic he reported: 'If I had not let the women go, they would have captured me, put me in a canoe and taken me off to be sacrificed.' And he added the information that one of the bridges on the causeway had been removed. All the causeways had bridges at intervals; the removal of the bridge on the Tacuba causeway meant that retreat from the city that way was cut off, an ominous sign. Cortés at once ordered a senior captain called de Ordás to take a strong party (400 men and most of the musketeers and crossbowmen) and reconnoitre the causeway. Hardly had he reached the main street when 'squadrons of Mexican soldiers fell on him and in the first assault killed eight soldiers and wounded the rest'. De Ordás, who was wounded in three places, had the greatest difficulty in fighting his way back. While this was happening in front, the Mexican army in strength attempted to rush the palace from the other sides, hurling javelins, slinging stones, and shooting arrows. The Spaniards, after suffering heavy casualties, managed to repulse the assault with their cannon and muskets, though the Mexicans broke in at points and fierce hand-to-hand fighting took place. The battle continued all day and unexpectedly did not cease altogether at night.

The next morning Cortés tried a sortie in force. 'I do not know how to describe the Mexicans' tenacity,' says Bernal. 'Neither cannon nor crossbows nor muskets availed, nor hand-to-hand fighting nor killing thirty or forty every time we charged. For they still fought on in closed ranks and with more energy than in the beginning. . . . That day they killed ten or twelve more of our soldiers and we all returned badly wounded.'

During the night work was begun on some wooden towers which could be wheeled into the streets and would enable the Spaniards to get at the Mexicans who fought with stones from the flat roofs. The third day was spent completing these towers and repulsing furious attacks. On the fourth day they sallied out with the towers. But the ground was too difficult. The city was cut up by innumerable canals which could not be crossed as the bridges were destroyed. And there was no definite objective. All Cortés could hope to do was to break the Mexicans' spirit. But in this he wholly failed. 'They showed themselves far more vigorous and employed greater forces on this day than before,' says Bernal. A raid was made on the gods whose shrines were on the great temple pyramid, but though the Spaniards reached the top and set fire to the shrines (the image of the Virgin was no longer there), they were driven down again, and, after losing sixteen men killed, hardly managed to get back behind their walls. All the towers were destroyed.

On the fifth morning, when the Mexicans renewed the assault

with the same fury as before, Cortés perceived that a few more days of such intense fighting would so fatigue his troops and reduce their numbers that the Mexicans would break in. The soldiers of Narváez's army had already begun to lose their nerve. He decided to ask for an armistice and to promise, if it were granted, to leave the city at once. His position was desperate. Even if he succeeded in repulsing the attacks, he could not endure a siege as he had no food.

Instead of trying to get in touch with Cuitlahuac, Cortés decided to ask Montezuma to negotiate a truce for him. As he was conceding the main point by offering to go, a truce ought to be possible to arrange. It was true that he had promised several times to go and had broken his promise. Even so, he thought Montezuma would be able to manage it. It is doubtful whether he had yet heard of Cuitlahuac's election. But Montezuma had heard of it and knew he had been deposed largely because he had failed to get the Spaniards to leave. He had been fatally discredited by Cortés' return and evident intention not to sail on the ships he had captured from Narváez. And for the first time he despaired.

Bernal, who had an instinctive feeling for relevant detail, though he was never able to give a precise explanation in words of the esoteric drama of which he was an eye-witness, records Montezuma's answer to Cortés' request. He says: 'When they went to give the message from Cortés to the Great Montezuma, it is reported that he said with deep grief: "What more does Malintzin want from me? I neither wish to live nor to listen to him, to such a pass has my fate brought me because of him." He did not want to come, and it is even reported that he neither wished to see nor hear him, nor listen to his false words, promises and lies.'

Cortés then sent the Padre de la Merced, the subtle priest who had made a fool of Narváez. The Padre succeeded in persuading Montezuma to speak to the besieging host whose shouts could be heard as they strove to break in and whose missiles were raining in the courtyard. But though he consented to speak, he declared it would be useless. He said: 'I cannot get them to stop fighting with you, for they have elected another sovereign and are resolved you shall not leave the city alive.'

There is an old tradition that Montezuma, before emerging to speak to his people on what was destined to be the last occasion, put on full official dress. If he did so, this consisted of a rich loin-cloth with long flaps, an embroidered mantle with a fringe, sandals with golden soles, a diadem with a plume, arm ornaments of gold, feathers and jade, a golden necklace, turquoise ear-plugs, a jade ornament piercing both nostrils and a crystal tube containing the feather of a kingfisher, which pierced his lower lip and stuck out above his chin. His face would also have been painted. So bizarre an official dress sounds barbaric to us, but was probably very beautiful, each of the articles comprising it being of exquisite workmanship, their colours of high quality and combined to perfection. The Spaniards very much admired costumes of the sort.

In some such splendid guise, if not dressed exactly so, Montezuma left his apartments and mounted the wall. Stones, darts and arrows were flying through the air and to protect him Spanish soldiers were detailed to cover him with their shields. When the Mexican leaders recognized the great personage whom until a few days before they would not have dared to look in the face, they ordered their troops to cease the attack and themselves approached to within speaking distance. Montezuma addressed them affectionately, begging them to fight no more, for it was unnecessary, since the Spaniards would now leave the country for a certainty. As they gazed up at him so grave, so dignified in his age and so sorrowful, they began to weep, and weeping replied: 'Great Lord of ours, we feel deeply for you in your misfortune. But we have had to elect another to be our Lord. Forgive us. We pray for you every day. When all is done and we have destroyed those whom the gods have ordered us to destroy, we shall pay you yet greater respect than before.'

The Death of Montezuma

Bernal says that during this colloquy on the wall the soldiers guarding Montezuma lowered their shields as there seemed no danger. Suddenly a volley of stones was flung at him. Who the slingers were, whether they were aiming at him or not, whether they were ordered to sling or did so of their own motion, is not known, though many guesses have been made. Three of the stones hit Montezuma, one of them on the head. He was carried to his apartments. It did not seem at first that he was mortally wounded. But he was suffering from severe shock, not only the physical shock of the wound but the psychic shock of his own misery. Bernal says that he refused food and would not let them dress his wounds. The next day it was evident that he was sinking. The Padre de la Merced made great efforts to convert him to Christianity, efforts which were followed with anxiety by the Spaniards, who, as they loved him, wished to save him from eternal damnation. But these ministrations were unavailing. It has been supposed that he thought of Christianity as having some connection with what Quetzalcoatl had taught on his former visit to earth. But in stating as much one is aware of the grave deficiency of one's knowledge. Without a much greater insight into Montezuma's mind than we possess it would be impossible to say what precisely were the objections that made it so hard for him to accept the creed brought by one, whom science, astrology, augury, magic proved was a member of the Mexican pantheon. It may have been that he could not make head or tail of it.

Cortés visited Montezuma before his death and promised to look after his three legitimate daughters, a promise he kept, for afterwards he had them married with suitable dowries to Spanish noblemen. The death took place on the fifth day of the siege, June 29th. 'When we least expected they came to say he was dead,' writes Bernal. 'Cortés wept for him and all of us captains and soldiers. There was not one of those of us who had known him intimately that did not lament him as if he were our father. And that was no wonder, considering how good he was.' Such is Bernal's simple epitaph.

That the mystery of Montezuma's life and death is fully explained here has been disavowed, but at least we have a notion of him as a man 'learned, an astrologer and a philosopher', the description already quoted from the *Codex Mendoza*, who, confronted by events which all his erudition told him inevitably led to the ruin of his race, did not give up hope and strove amid humiliations and increasing despair to find a solution.

It is a mistake to think of him as deluded because he used a vocabulary and a set of concepts, which belonged to magic and mythology, to account for the apparition of Cortés. Could he have seen the fateful landing on the coast as an invasion in the ordinary sense and taken the ordinary measures to repulse it, he might have been successful for a while. But the landing of Cortés was far more than an ordinary invasion. It was a world event which in the long run was certain to be irresistible and fatal. Montezuma could no more have prevented the incursion of Europe than he could have stopped the march of time. That his gods and his country's independence were doomed to wither away was part and parcel of a global event, Europe's domination of the world, which was ushered in by Christopher Columbus and Vasco da Gama and was destined to continue for four centuries. No wonder such an event was foreshadowed in the subconscious minds of the Mexicans and assumed the form of a transcendental cataclysm.

Had Montezuma seen nothing in Cortés' landing but a foreign invasion there would be ground for dismissing his occult sciences as a delusion, but since they indicated correctly the landing's essential nature, which was more than did any body of ideas then current in Europe, we cannot dismiss them as a hallucination. In a broad view Montezuma had more insight into the fundamental reality of what was happening than had Cortés. And that he had this glimpse of the essence of what fate was bringing forth makes him the leading protagonist.

The Death of Montezuma

But his practice of human sacrifice so revolts us that we have difficulty in conceding his greatness. So utterly was he lacking in compassion when engaged in placating and sustaining the gods, that further back the exclamation escaped that he was a monster. Yet how inadequate to explain his character has that first judgment become! His ritual inhumanities are seen to be religious mysteries. He seems to take leave of mankind and enter mythology. In the super-real he rises up like an image of a pitiless universe. In this way he resembles the masterpieces of Mexican art.

'The Great Montezuma', writes Bernal again and again, who saw him every day for over six months, saw him despair and saw him die. Among the many figures in the old Spaniard's book no other man is called great; no other man made such an impression. As we can never know him half as well as did Bernal, we had better take his word for it that Montezuma was a great man. With him gone the story loses its richness. Not that dramatic incident is lacking. The most exciting adventures are to come. But the Mexican leaders seem no more than heroic boys after the strange king who with such devoted patience sought to escape a dilemma which passed understanding.

⟨22⟩

Cortés Flees from Mexico City

Cortés handed over the body of Montezuma to the Mexicans for burial. 'When they beheld him thus dead, we saw their tears and heard their cries of grief,' says Bernal. But soon afterwards 'they fell on us in greater force and fury, with loud yells and whistles and showers of missiles, shouting: "Now for certain you will pay for his death. In two days there will not be one of you left."'

Having failed to secure a truce Cortés decided to try and fight his way out of the city. 'We saw our forces diminishing,' says Bernal, 'and those of the Mexicans increasing. Many of our men were dead and all the rest wounded. The powder was giving out and so was the food and water. And the Great Montezuma was dead. In fact we were staring death in the face.'

A certain Botello, however, gave them hope. He was, says Bernal, 'apparently an honest man and a Latin scholar, who had been in Rome. Some said he was a magician, some that he had a familiar spirit, others called him an astrologer.' Cortés had consulted him on his horoscope and was told that though he would have a serious setback at this time, later he would become 'a great and magnificent lord'. Botello now advised the Spaniards to leave on the night of June 30th, declaring that if they did so, his calculations showed that they would be lucky.

If they delayed, not one of them would get out alive. His recommended date, which was the next day, was therefore fixed for the flight.

The best way of getting out of the city was by the Tacuba causeway as it was the shortest. There were eight bridges in its length of two miles, and all of them had been destroyed. But Cortés devised an answer to this by having a portable bridge built. They would carry this with them in their rush for the mainland and bridge the gaps in succession. The whole of June 29th, the day Montezuma died, and the following morning were spent in making the portable bridge; also in sorties to try and secure the approach to the causeway, and even in attempting to fill some of the gaps in it with rubble. It must not be forgotten that besides the Tlaxcalan contingent of soldiers the Spaniards had with them many servants, porters and labourers, who now came in very handy. The Tlaxcalans were useful as auxiliaries, but were not trained enough to be incorporated into the Spanish formations, which, small as they were, had a cohesion which greatly increased their strength. This cohesion had been created by discipline and improved by battle experience. The Spanish at this date were at the height of their reputation as soldiers. A body of their troops showed the mobile unity and intelligent co-operation of the legion or the phalanx in their best days. But the legion and the phalanx could only survive against a certain degree of odds, and the odds now looked too heavy for the Spaniards. Moreover, only Cortés' original army was fully trained and first class; the new-comers lacked nerve and confidence.

It remained to settle about the treasure before they left. Though everyone had been allotted his share, only part had been drawn. The bulk remained for safety in a strong-room. It was now mostly in the form of ingots, though there was some gold jewellery which had not been melted down and other valuables like jades. Even after the heavy expense of buying over Narváez's officers and men, the value of it is given as over

700,000 pieces of gold. On the late afternoon of the 30th, some hours before the time fixed for the flight, the whole was heaped up in the main hall. Cortés first separated the Emperor's Fifth in gold ingots and entrusted it to two captains, who were given eight wounded horses and a party of eighty Tlaxcalans to transport it. He then addressed the troops. 'I can do no more with the rest,' said he. 'It is all yours. Take what you think you can carry away.'

Death might be round the corner, but these men, who had come to Mexico to make a fortune and saw a fortune on the floor, forgot about death. Not caring whether to be loaded with gold was a safe way to go into a desperate battle, many of them, particularly the Narváez lot, for whom it was the first sight of treasure, stuffed their pockets, even packed their helmets. Bernal was more cautious: 'I declare that I had no other desire than to save my life,' he confides, and says he selected some jades which he secreted between his chest and his armour. 'Later on, what I was able to sell them for helped me to get my wounds attended to and to buy me food.' How much Cortés took for himself is unrecorded. No doubt before the heap was put out in the hall he had reserved as much as his own staff of servants and porters could manage.

When darkness fell they got ready to make their escape. The order was as follows: Sandoval and Ordás were to lead the van with a company of picked men. Cortés would command the centre and lend support where it was most needed. Alvarado took the place of most danger, the rearguard. The cannon, which had to be carried, and the Emperor's Fifth, were to go in the centre, as were the prisoner lords, including Lord Maize Cobs. Some women were taken, the most important being Doña Marina, Doña Luisa, the daughter of the senior lord of Tlaxcala, who was Alvarado's consort, and two of Montezuma's daughters—not the same girls as those he mentioned on his death-bed. A son of his was also with the Spaniards.

A little before midnight the evacuation began. There was

some moon, but as rain was falling, it was tolerably dark. They were not observed, it seems, for a short while, but by the time the van had reached the head of the causeway and the portable bridge was being shoved over the first gap, 'the trumpets and whistles of the Mexicans began to sound', and soon afterwards strong forces charged them. Canoes of armed men also rowed out and landed further down the causeway so as to cut them off.

Though they were certainly at a great disadvantage, being surrounded on all sides and not able to use their strongest weapon, the artillery, as it was being carried, they had this advantage that the Mexicans on account of the narrowness of the causeway could not bring their greatly superior forces to bear. They tried to deploy, by attacking from canoes on both flanks, but there also large numbers could not be effectively used. Nevertheless, only the greatest coolness and discipline could extricate a small force from such a position in face of charges relentlessly pushed by a fighting people of the calibre of the Mexicans and as well armed with missile weapons.

What happened is described at length by Bernal and more shortly by Cortés in his letter to the Emperor. The van and part of the centre, with Cortés among them, had crossed the portable bridge when it was destroyed by the Mexicans. This stroke cut the Spanish army in half. The hinder part, together with most of the Emperor's Fifth, the prisoner lords, all the cannon and some of the women, was left on the Mexico side of the gap. Cortés had to take an immediate decision—whether to stay and try to extricate those cut off or lead the men with him down the causeway before it was too late. If he had stayed, there is little doubt, I think, that he and the entire army would have perished. Instead, with his mailed cavalry in front like a battering-ram, he forced a passage through, swimming his men and horses over the seven other gaps or, if narrow or shallow enough, jumping or wading them. Bernal, who was with him, is here emphatic: 'I assert that if we had waited, not one of us would have been left alive.' On getting some five hundred of his men safely to Tacuba, Cortés turned back with a few horsemen and foot soldiers to see if he could rescue those left on the far side of the first bridge. After going a certain distance, he met Alvarado walking towards him. He was badly wounded and accompanied by a handful of men. He informed Cortés that everyone else had either been killed or captured. All the guns had been taken and the bulk of the treasure. The captive lords had been killed in the mêlée, including Lord Maize Cobs. De León also and many other notable gentlemen were dead. He himself had got across the fatal gap by clambering over the dead bodies, horses and boxes which filled it. On hearing this terrible news, Cortés, perceiving it was useless to go on returned with Alvarado and his remnant to Tacuba. Bernal adds a few details. Of Botello he says: 'His astrology availed him nothing, for he too died there with his horse.' Of the horses, twenty-three survived out of eighty. The Tlaxcalan contingent had been badly mauled: Montezuma's son and two daughters were killed. And he says. 'Of the followers of Narváez the greater number were left at the bridge weighed down with gold.' There was only one bright spot: 'How happy we were to see Doña Marina still alive, and Doña Luisa, whose escape at the bridge was due to some Tlaxcalans, and also another women called Maria de Estrada, who was the only Spanish woman in Mexico.' Of this intrepid female nothing else is known.

The flight had so far cost Cortés more than half of his army. 'It was a miracle that any of us escaped,' he wrote. And they were only at Tacuba, still in sight of the city. Most of them were wounded. The Mexican army was intact. A pursuit was inevitable. Where were they to go? The country-side was roused against them. They could never reach the coast. It seemed, indeed, that, if any were to escape, another miracle would be required. By miracle, Cortés meant a real miracle—the personal intervention of God or His Saints.

$\mathcal{E}23\mathcal{E}$

The Magical Battle of Otumba

When Cortés got back to Tacuba with Alvarado he found his men in a panic, he says. Some Mexican troops had come up and were attacking them, as were the soldiers stationed in the town. It seems that a Tlaxcalan told him of a pyramid temple about four miles away in a hill town called Totoltepec (The Hill of the Turkey Hen). We have seen how these pyramid temples made good fortresses. Cortés resolved to march there at once. His men and horses were very exhausted, but he managed the retreat so skilfully that in spite of a harassing pursuit there were no more losses. After dawn Mexican troops arrived and tried to take the temple-courtyard. They continued to attack all day. The Spaniards, bandaged and starving, were in a desperate state, yet succeeded in beating them off. Nevertheless, the situation seemed bound to get worse. The main body of the Mexicans had not appeared so far; when it did the end would come.

Cortés, however, had his plan. The Tlaxcalans had proved themselves faithful allies. If the Spaniards could reach Tlaxcala they might find sanctuary there. But it was about a hundred miles away. Could they fight a rearguard action all that distance? Moreover, he was not certain of their reception. He wrote: 'We were not quite positive of finding the Tlaxcalans friendly. Seeing us so reduced, they might decide to kill us in order to recover the independence they had once enjoyed.' It was indeed a question. So far the Tlaxcalans had helped the Spaniards against the Mexicans, even though a Spanish victory would mean Spanish domination over the whole country. Would they now think better of such an alliance? On the whole Cortés felt they would not desert him, such was their hatred of the Mexicans. To get to them, however, remained the problem. He resolved to set out that very night.

Leaving fires burning to deceive the enemy, the Spaniards left the Hill of the Turkey Hen at midnight. Soon after daylight their pursuers came up with them. But it was not the main army. For some reason the Mexicans were not following up their victory on the causeway with the full forces at their disposal. What could be the meaning of this?

The probable explanation is that they were busy sacrificing to the Humming Bird the Spaniards whom they had captured. The number captured is unknown. Bernal gives the total loss on the causeway and on the march to Tlaxcala at over eight hundred men. As the Mexican tactics were always to capture rather than to kill, some hundreds are likely to have been available for sacrifice. The ritual of so important a god-feast may well have required a temporary cessation of hostilities. The soldiers who had taken the captives would have had to be present and what with the dancing and the eating of the bodies the festival would have lasted some days. Bernal records the threats which the Mexicans shouted at them a day or so before the flight: 'We will sacrifice your hearts and blood to our gods and there will be enough of you to glut their appetites. We will feast on your arms and legs, and throw your bodies to the serpents and carnivora, which are very hungry because we have not fed them for two days on purpose.' War in Mexico, as explained earlier, was closely connected with religion. If in this case the correct procedure of sacrifice so required, the pursuit would have had to be postponed. The soldiers would not have thought religion was interfering with strategy. The religious reason for postponing the pursuit would have seemed also a military one. If the magical liturgy was carried through correctly, the Humming Bird, revived and indulgent, would give them victory. If it was neglected, no strategy, however apparently sound, would be effectual.

But if this was the reason why the Commander-in-Chief, whose title it will be recalled was the Serpent Woman, did not order an immediate pursuit by the whole of his command and left it for the time being to local forces to harry the Spaniards as they fled, he was mistaken in thinking that he had the magical texts on his side, for his original misreading of them was fatal and he had already signed his own death warrant, as the sequel was to show. Montezuma had given the correct reading: any attack on Cortés-Quetzalcoatl would result in the destruction of the country. The Commander-in-Chief as a member of the council who had elected Cuitlahuac had been partly responsible for amending Montezuma's reading. That vitiated all the rest. No amount of captives, no matter how correctly they were sacrificed, could abate the fatal consequences of such a fundamental error.

The route taken in their flight by the Spaniards was round the north shore of the lake, the same road that they had recently traversed when marching in from Tetzcuco. They would be branching off it, however, fourteen miles north of that city and would make straight for Tlaxcala via Otumba. Though battered and famished, their valour was undiminished. Bernal gives the moving picture: 'The Tlaxcalans went cautiously in front as guides. We marched with the wounded in the middle, the lame walking with sticks, the badly wounded on the croups of horses too lame to fight. The horsemen who were unwounded covered the flanks. The less wounded of us kept our faces to the enemy who harassed us with loud cries and whistles.' In this way, warding off stones, arrows and javelins with their shields, and sometimes having to repulse charges, they marched for six days, and on July 7th reached the plain before Otumba, distant forty miles from Tlaxcala.

The Commander-in-Chief had taken his army across the lake to Tetzcuco and marched it the fifteen miles to Otumba. There he was awaiting the arrival of the Spaniards with 'the flower of Mexico and Tetzcuco and the towns around the lake, who all came in the belief that not a trace of us would be left. There had never been seen throughout the Indies such a great number of fighting men in any battle,' says Bernal.

The Spaniards suddenly came upon this host. Turning a corner of a hill their scouts descried it covering the plain a few miles away. Cortés, who had been wounded in the head and in his left hand, but had not given in to pain and weariness, halted his men, who were straggling along, and told them the news. 'When we heard this, we were indeed alarmed, but did not lose our nerve. We were ready to meet them and fight to the death,' says Bernal. Cortés drew them up in battle formation and re-minded them of the tactics used in the battles when, in numbers approximately the same, they had successfully resisted the big Tlaxcalan army. He said that the horsemen should charge in squads of five, aim at the face, and return at a hand gallop; the soldiers should then attack the enemy disordered by the charge and were to thrust rather than cut. They should make a point of seeking out and killing the leading Mexicans, easily distin-guished by their gorgeous accoutrements, plumes, banners which were attached to their backs, mantles with devices, face jewels and headdresses in the form of serpents and ocelots. He called on his men for a supreme effort, though, as he afterwards re-ported to Charles, 'we were already exhausted, and almost all of us were wounded and fainting from hunger'.

In this mood of desperate valour they advanced into the plain. The *Codex Mendoza*, one of the few Mexican manu-scripts which have survived, has drawings of many varieties of the uniforms in use at this time. As a sartorial display the Mexican army must have been a spectacle of colour and fantasy surpassing the Field of the Cloth of Gold. But what followed was far from a pageant. 'They attacked us on all sides so violently,' wrote Cortés, 'that we could not distinguish each other, for being so pressed and entangled with them. We spent a great part of the day in this struggle, until it pleased God that one of those persons, who must have been an important leader, fell, and with his death all the battle ceased.' This personage was no less than the Serpent Woman himself. Bernal is more explicit on this matter. After writing: 'Oh, what a sight it was this fearful and destructive battle! We moved all mixed up with them, foot to foot. The thrusts we gave them! With what fury the dogs fought! What wounds and death they inflicted on us with their lances and their two-handed swords!' he goes on to describe a charge led by Cortés. With him, it seems, were all his captains, as formidable in their mail and on their mailed horses as is a tank among infantry to-day. 'They reached the place where the Captain General of the Mexicans was marching with his banner displayed, wearing rich golden armour and great gold and silver plumes. Cortés struck his horse against him. However, it was Juan de Salamanca, riding with Cortés on a good piebald mare, who gave him a lance thrust and took from him the rich plumes that he wore. On the death of that captain all their attack slackened.'

In old battles the death of the leader was often such a moral shock to his troops that they lost the heart to go on fighting. In this battle the fall of the Serpent Woman was far more than a moral shock. It was a sign that there had been a mistake in the magico-religious calculations on whose correctness the issue depended. The Mexicans could not tell where the mistake lay. It was more difficult to find than would be an error in a page of modern equations, because there was an unknown element, the magical counter measures which Cortés-Quetzalcoatl must have used. Cortés himself attributed his victory to Christ: 'Our Lord was pleased to show His great power and mercy to us, for despite our weakness we broke their great pride.' Bernal is as

The Magical Battle of Otumba

emphatic and fuller: 'Our Lord Jesus Christ and our Lady the Virgin Mary gave us courage and St. James certainly aided us.' The Mexicans, whose system was more elaborate and mechanical, did not think that Cortés had been saved by the intervention of divinities, but because, as a divine apparition himself, he had a reserve of magical secrets and had been able to manipulate them in the confusing cosmic play of forces which was the universe, in such a way as to checkmate the magical measures they had taken. If Montezuma had been alive he would not have been surprised at their discomfiture. They had gone against his opinion that, from the magical point of view, it was a mistake to try to overcome Cortés by force. That being a fundamental governing factor, all their subsequent calculations were in the air. So, to the question—how did the Spaniards manage to be victorious at Otumba?—the answer is—because the Mexicans thought themselves beaten.

From Otumba the hills surrounding Tlaxcala were visible, a glad sight. The Spaniards marched on, satisfying their hunger on maize, cooked or roasted, on melons and on the flesh of a horse that was killed in battle. Some regiments of the enemy followed, but did not attack. The next day they crossed the Tlaxcalan frontier and rested in safety. Bernal gives their numbers at this time as 440 men, with 20 horses, 12 crossbows and 7 muskets. They had no powder left and were covered with wounds. It was still uncertain whether the Tlaxcalan federation would receive them, though its contingent had supported them so bravely throughout. The federal army, which as we know was the largest in the country after the Mexican, had not come to their assistance. If this meant that the Tlaxcalans were no no longer friendly and intended to attack them in their weakness, they had little chance of survival. But on the day following, July 9th, the leading men of the federation arrived and bade them an affectionate welcome. After embracing Cortés, they said, weeping: 'Oh, Malintzin! Malintzin! how grieved we are at your misfortunes, and at the number of our people who have been killed with yours. But it cannot be helped and now we must feed you up and take care of you. We have quarters ready for you at Tlaxcala.' And they told him that if they had admired him before, their admiration was now much greater, seeing that he had escaped from Mexico, that impregnable city, and been victorious at Otumba. As for their not having marched to his assistance, he must excuse them for that; they had not had time to mobilize.

Cortés, who knew the knack of responding gracefully to such advances, joined in their tears, embraced them again and distributed little trifles from what remains of Montezuma's treasure he had managed to bring through. In a day or so they all left for Tlaxcala and in that comfortable city, where nothing was lacking but salt and cotton, their wounds were cared for and they were bountifully fed.

€24å

Cortés Recuperates at Tlaxcala

It may seem clear enough why the Tlaxcalans welcomed back the Spaniards: they hated the Mexicans, they were sworn allies of Cortés. But this is too great a simplification. It suggests they were so short-sighted that they were ready to surrender their independence in order to be avenged on the Mexicans. But could they have been so muddle-headed? To defeat an enemy but lose to a friend the very thing they were fighting the enemy to retain, would have been too stupid.

The true explanation is that the Tlaxcalans had from the beginning an overriding motive for submitting to the Spaniards. When Cortés had first marched in from the coast, they had tested him to ascertain whether he was the divinity he was alleged to be, and they came to the conclusion that he was. Since that was so, prophecy declared him the future ruler of the country. He would become the ruler, whether they helped him or not. In joining him as allies, they were not surrendering their independence, for that was fated to end, but insuring a favoured treatment for themselves. So firmly were they convinced of his divinity, that the sight of him famished and battered on their frontier did not affect his reputation. What he had achieved in Mexico, Montezuma's surrender to him, the whole extraordinary adventure, had been followed by them with the greatest admiration. No one had denied his identity with Quetzalcoatl.

His misfortunes were of a passing kind. He would continue and prove the prophecy correct. It was delightful that he had appealed to them for help. His entry into Mexico without the army they had offered him had been a great disappointment. Now he would have use for their army; they would earn his gratitude and, when all others suffered tribulation, they would profit by his indulgence.

The Tlaxcalan assumption that Cortés would return to Mexico at the head of their army no doubt influenced him in coming to a decision on his next step. When in defeat he was fleeing for shelter to Tlaxcala, the best he could have hoped for was to reach the coast in safety. Now at Tlaxcala he was in a much stronger position than had he gone to Vera Cruz. To get at him the Mexicans would have to undertake the full scale invasion of an independent state. If the Tlaxcalans had always been able to repulse such invasions by themselves, with his assistance the task would be yet easier. His communications with Vera Cruz were intact. He could obtain reinforcements and military stores. His great weakness was the loss of his money. However, he had saved something of Montezuma's treasure. Given time he saw ways of rebuilding his strength. His original objection to using the Tlaxcalan army no longer was valid. He would not be representing himself henceforth as a peaceful envoy of Charles V. His re-entry into Mexican territory would be that of an undisguised invader. To take the capital by assault would be a great feat of arms, but with the Tlaxcalan army it should not be impossible. In a broad view he saw that his position was sounder now, because better defined, than it had been when, both Montezuma's gaoler and his prisoner, he never knew from one day to another precisely how he stood.

What occurred between the arrival of the Spaniards at Tlaxcala on 12th July 1520 and their departure for Mexico on December 28th, five and a half months later, can be shortly given. After about a month in Tlaxcala, by which time most of his men had recovered from their wounds, Cortés thought it essential to strengthen his lines of communication with the coast. On the Orizaba route, the shortest and best, there were some towns with Mexican garrisons. Spaniards going by this route had been robbed and killed. He decided to seize the towns. Marching from Tlaxcala with all his men and 2,000 Tlaxcalan auxiliaries, he made a sudden descent and took them. To secure the route for the future he built a fortified post which he called Segura de la Frontera. From there he raided certain other Mexican towns south of the route. Satisfied that he could now bring up men and supplies from Vera Cruz without risk, he returned to Tlaxcala to make his preparations for invading the valley of Mexico.

During this time some events of importance had occurred. Smallpox, hitherto unknown in Mexico, broke out. The infection had been introduced by a negro in Narváez's army. A terrible epidemic was the result. Thousands of Mexicans died, including Montezuma's successor Cuitlahuac. The severity of the epidemic, the death of the head of the state, and the highly ominous character of such disasters explain why the Mexicans were less active against Cortés than might have been expected. Cuitlahuac was succeeded by Quauhtemoctzin (Lord Falling Eagle). Bernal describes him as 'a young man of about twenty-five years, very much of a gentleman and extremely brave. His wife was one of Montezuma's daughters, a very pretty woman.'

Between August and November 1520, several ships called at Vera Cruz, some sent for Narváez by Velázquez, who did not yet know that he was Cortés' prisoner. They contained men, horses, powder, etc. The authorities at Vera Cruz seized each in turn and sent Cortés the men and everything else of use on board. By further good luck a large ship arrived from Spain, a private trading venture. It carried quantities of powder, muskets, and crossbows. In this case Cortés bought the entire cargo. These windfalls raised his army to nearly five hundred and supplied it with munitions of war.

The money required for this purchase, as well as heavy expenses which Cortés incurred by sending envoys to the Viceregal court in Hispaniola, and fresh envoys to the court of Spain, leads Bernal to make some sarcastic remarks about his methods of raising funds. He accuses him of forcing his poor soldiers to disgorge the gold which he had allowed them to take from the heap of treasure at the last moment in Mexico. Bernal had a tremendous admiration for his Captain-General as a commander in the field, but thought him downright mean where money was concerned. Cortés, however, had to have money to carry on the conquest. That he was able to get it out of his men shows they still believed that he would make them rich in the end. When the conquest was over, Bernal found himself still a poor man, but Cortés had become enormously wealthy. Bernal's complaint, constantly repeated, is that had it not been for the indomitable valour and endurance of the rank and file, Cortés could have done nothing. But grumbling of this sort is characteristic of old soldiers, and we like Bernal the better for it.

As part of his plan for the campaign against Mexico, Cortés directed that timber be felled for building thirteen sloops. The Mexicans had thousands of canoes. We have seen how they harassed the Spaniards on the causeways. They also served to provision the city and carry troops to the mainland. Cortés regarded sloops as the answer to the canoes. He had an excellent shipwright. Nails and tools were sent for to Vera Cruz. The Tlaxcalans provided the labour and offered to carry the sloops in sections the fifty miles to Tetzcuco, where they could be fitted together and launched. At this time one of the senior lords of the federation died of smallpox. There had been some dissensions in the Council on how far to support Cortés, and this old lord on his death-bed solemnly warned his colleagues that to withhold support would be a grave error. Bernal makes him say: 'You must always be most careful to do what Malintzin tells you, for he is certainly the one destined by fate to govern the country.'

Cortés Recuperates at Tlaxcala

Accordingly, when in the latter part of December 1520 Cortés declared his intention of re-entering the valley of Mexico, the federation placed a contingent of 10,000 men at his disposal. A review was held and on the day after Christmas the army marched to its first objective, the capture of Tetzcuco on the great lake. The number of Spanish soldiers is given by Cortés as 40 horse and 450 foot, the latter including 80 crossbowmen and musketeers. There were 8 or 9 field guns. The sloops were to be sent when ready.

$\{25\}$

Cortés Beleaguers Mexico City

Mexico was reputed to be an impregnable city. But there is no such thing nor ever has been. Every city can be stormed if you find out how to do it. Cortés had been thinking over the problem. If he seized the towns at the foot of the causeways, no food or supplies could enter the city except by canoe. If his sloops commanded the waters of the lake, the canoe traffic would be stopped. The city's water supply could also be cut off. It was carried on an aqueduct from Chapultepec (The Hill of the Grasshopper), a town on the mainland a short distance south of Tacuba. After investing the city in this way, he planned to advance up the three causeways simultaneously. With his flanks covered by the sloops and his rear resting on the towns on shore, he ought to be capable of forcing his way in. The causeways varied in breadth, but in general eight horsemen could advance abreast. He calculated that on so narrow a front his musketeers, cannon and crossbowmen would be able to mow down the packed Mexican forces. The mailed cavalry could then charge and the swordsmen follow and methodically secure the passage.

Before going against the towns at the foot of the causeways, he had first to take Tetzcuco and launch his sloops. To reach it there was a high pass to cross in the range that enclosed that part of the valley of Mexico. The Mexicans had not believed at first that he would return, but when it appeared that he intended to do so, they began to prepare counter measures. Among others they blocked the pass over the range by felling trees at the narrowest gorges. Cortés was afraid that part of their army would be waiting there in ambush. But the pass was not held and his army crossed without opposition. As they advanced down the slopes towards Tetzcuco, they were met by a deputation with a golden banner. Its leader knelt and said that he had been sent to welcome them peaceably to the city. The ruler of Tetzcuco was no longer the Lord Swallow whom Cortés had placed there to succeed Lord Maize Cobs, but his brother, a nominee of Lord Falling Eagle's. Somewhat surprised by the message of goodwill, Cortés replied very cordially to the deputation and promised that no harm would be done to the citizens.

On his arrival at Tetzcuco no women and children were to be seen, an indication that something was afoot. Alvarado climbed to the top of the tallest pyramid and saw crowds of people leaving with bundles. It turned out that the deputation had been sent to give the Mexicans time to remove everything of value. The Lord himself had fled to Mexico. However, the upshot was that the Spaniards gained Tetzcuco, the second largest city in the valley, without having to strike a blow. Their sudden crossing of the mountains had evidently taken the Mexicans by surprise. Bernal attributes this partly to the smallpox which had been ravaging the valley.

Cortés' first act was to appoint a new Lord. He chose the son of Lord Maize Cob's predecessor. The young man was given Spanish tutors and shortly afterwards was baptized, taking Cortés' names with the prefix of Don. This calmed the inhabitants, who thenceforth sided with the Spaniards.

The readiness of the Tetzcucoans, once the Mexicans had gone, to settle down under the Spaniards, was characteristic of the instability of the Mexican empire. All its subject cities and peoples were more or less disaffected. Nevertheless, they would not have sided with Cortés had they not been convinced that he was the conqueror foretold by divine prophecy.

Tetzcuco was about two miles from the lake shore. Cortés could have had the sloops assembled near the water, but he thought it would be safer in the city. A canal to float them to the lake had therefore to be dug. While the timber was being sawn into the required shapes at Tlaxcala and the canal excavated at Tetzcuco, he occupied the time by a careful reconnaissance of the approaches to Mexico and a methodical reduction of the garrisons which the Mexicans had in the neighbourhood. Several of the towns joined him, as soon as the garrisons were driven out, and promised him contingents for the assault on the city. He calculated that, if he wished, he could build up an auxiliary army of 100,000 men. He had begun to train the Tlaxcalans in European tactics, making them more amenable to discipline and showing them how they could best support him in battle. He hoped to be able to do the same with the rest. But the military science of the country turned so much on securing captives for sacrifice, and was so bound up with augury and magic, that it would be no easy task to substitute common sense. He was to succeed up to a point, though he found it impossible to instil the idea of clemency, for mercy in war was unknown in those parts. His auxiliaries never became like the native regiments created by the British in India. What they and their followers were like is disclosed in the following passage from Bernal: 'Many of them came in hope of spoil. They also came to gorge on human flesh. It was like in Italy. There an army on the march is followed by crows and kites and other birds of prey, which live on the dead bodies left on the battlefield.' As these sinister allies were indispensable to Cortés, he had to put up with their horrible practices. In his letters to the Emperor he frequently deplores them, as does Bernal in his chronicle. The truth is that once the rot set in against the Mexicans, and all their subject peoples in the valley turned against them, Cortés had more allies than he wanted and could manage. To be the commander of an avenging cannibal host was very distasteful to him. He took every opportunity of trying to persuade Lord Falling Eagle to acknowledge Charles V and accept a peace that would have preserved the city and the lives of its inhabitants. But as we shall see the Mexicans preferred a fight to the death as according best with their conception of life.

Both Cortés and Bernal cover many pages in describing the military operations preliminary to the assault upon the city. As soldiers the subject interested them and was easier to grasp than the mysterious relations with Montezuma. We are given detailed accounts of skirmishes, the storming of towns, and hairbreadth escapes. Twice Cortés was nearly captured and taken to be sacrificed. To retail these adventures here is impossible; nor is it necessary for they are of minor importance. They occupied the months from January to May 1521. Cortés succeeded in destroying all the Mexican garrisons in the valley and its vicinity. He marched completely round the lake and set fire to those towns where, as sometimes happened, the inhabitants were pro-Mexican. By the time the sloops were finished, he was ready to enter the causeways. The Mexicans had fought furiously to break through the net he was weaving round them. They were near victory on two occasions and did him severe damage on several, but failed to concentrate at the right spot a force big enough to win a decisive victory. Lord Falling Eagle, though a brave man, seems to have been a timid general. He neglected to attack Tetzcuco when Cortés was away with the bulk of his army marching round the lake. He never sallied out with his whole army and challenged the Spaniards in a pitched battle. He had interior lines and could strike at any point; and his forces were greatly superior in numbers until Cortés had released the vassal towns and added their troops to his own. It looks as if the battle of Otumba had convinced him that however he chose his ground, however numerous his forces, and, yet more important, however apparently favourable were the omens, he would be defeated for reasons he did not know how to provide against. He therefore did not take a strategic offensive and spent his energies in a tactical defensive. It was as if he had already begun to despair. Montezuma had been deposed for not resisting fate. He was resisting fate. But could fate be resisted?

The sections of the sloops were carried to Tetzcuco some time in March or April by a line of porters six miles long. Sandoval, who was sent to Tlaxcala to escort them, had an unnerving experience at a temple he visited near the road. He saw in the shrine at the top of the pyramid two bearded faces on the altar. On closer inspection he found these to be of tanned skin. They had belonged to two of several Spaniards who had been captured, sacrificed and flayed. 'There was also found four tanned skins of horses with the hair on and the shoes.' The clothes of the Spaniards had also been offered to the god. Sandoval was shown the house where his compatriots had been kept before sacrifice and read on the wall: 'Here was imprisoned the unhappy Juan Juste with many others of his company', an inscription, as Cortés told the Emperor, 'fit without doubt to break the heart of those who saw it'. Such was the fate which all the Spaniards knew was inevitably theirs if they were captured. Further down I shall be quoting from Bernal, where he confesses how terrified he was of being sacrificed.

But to return to the arrival of the ships' timbers, 'a marvellous sight to see and it seems to me even to hear of', as Cortés put it in his letter to Charles. Besides Sandoval and his men, a large force of Tlaxcalans were guarding the porters and made a brave show as they entered the city in their best mantles and coloured plumes, marching to music and shouting: 'Long live the Emperor! Castille! Tlaxcala!' The boards, the planking, the ribs, the keels, were deposited beside the canal and the greatest despatch used in putting them together. To build a fleet in this way would anywhere have been thought original and in Mexico seemed astonishing. Cortés' ingenuity raised him far above his captains. Everyone knew, including Bernal, in spite of his insistence on the valour of the soldiery, that were Cortés to fall there was no one to take his place. To the Tlaxcalans and the many other peoples who joined him, his actions seemed to have the unpredictable singularity of the divinity that he was.

Nevertheless, a plot was hatched to assassinate him. Some of the followers of Narváez, though they had joined him, had never forgiven his defeat of their chief. Now one of them called Villafaña, a great friend of Velázquez's, planned with others to stab him at dinner. When the mail came in from Vera Cruz, Villafaña was to hasten to him with a letter, saying it was from his father, Martin Cortés, and while he was reading it, they would kill him. The Narváez party would then assume control. But the conspiracy leaked out. Cortés went quickly to Villafaña's lodging and had him seized. A paper was found on him with a list of the conspirators. He was brought to trial and sentenced to death. 'They hanged him from the window of a room where he had lodged,' says Bernal. The case was not pressed against the others, as the scandal would have been too great. After this the captains begged Cortés to have a bodyguard; alarmed for his safety, they were not unaware that theirs depended on it.

On 28th April 1521, after the sloops had been launched and 50,000 arrows made, Cortés held a review at Tetzcuco. Reinforcements had been coming up from Vera Cruz with the arrival of more ships. He now had 84 horsemen, 650 men-atarms, and 180 crossbowmen and musketeers. Each sloop required 25 men including those who managed the oars and sails, so that the force available for land operations was proportionately reduced. The land force was divided into three. One part under Sandoval was to occupy Iztapalapan and advance on Mexico by the southern causeway. A second division under Cristóbal de Olid was to occupy Coyuacan (Place of Many Lean Coyotes), a town west of Iztapalapan, from which two causeways ran out at different angles and joined the Iztapalapan causeway. The third division, under Alvarado, had orders to go west to Tacuba and use its causeway for the assault. The cutting of the aqueduct at Chapultepec nearby was to be its first task. The northern causeway from Tepeyacac (In the Beginning of the Hill) was not closed in the first phase of the operations. Each of the three commanders had about 200 Spanish soldiers and 8,000 auxiliaries. Cortés remained in command of the sloops, a central position which enabled him to oversee the three divisions. Bernal accompanied Alvarado and had apparently some subordinate command.

Sandoval, de Olid and Alvarado took up their positions between the 20th and 31st of May. The preliminary operations against the garrisons had been so successful that de Olid and Alvarado were able to march almost unopposed into Coyuacan and Tacuba. Alvarado immediately cut the water supply at Chapultepec. Sandoval had to fight before he could occupy Iztapalapan. It was off Iztapalapan that the fleet had its first action with the canoes. Cortés left Tetzcuco with the thirteen sloops to support Sandoval. He was sighted by watchers, who sent up smoke signals. Hundreds of canoes full of armed men issued from Mexico and bore down on him. At the moment he was lying off a small island. 'I ordered the captains of the sloops not to move,' he wrote afterwards to Charles, 'so as to induce the canoes to attack us in the belief that we were afraid of them. They came on till they were distant about two arrow-shots. It pleased Our Lord that when we were observing each other, a good land wind sprang up which enabled us to attack them. I immediately ordered the captains to break through the fleet. As the wind was strong we were quickly in the middle of them, though they fled as fast as they could. We destroyed an infinite number and killed and wounded many of their occupants. It was the greatest sight to be seen in the world. We pursued them fully nine miles, until we shut them up among the houses of the city. Thus it pleased Our Lord to give us the best and greatest victory which we could have asked or desired.'

This naval victory enabled Cortés to land on the Iztapalapan causeway at the point where the longer of the two causeways from Coyuacan joined it. The junction was about two miles from Mexico and seems to have been like a small island town, for there were two temples on it. There he established his head-quarters. Navigable gaps were made in the causeway so that the sloops could sail on both sides of it and prevent the Mexicans from landing troops by canoe in his rear. It became a safe road connecting him with Sandoval at Iztapalapan and by the branch with Olid at Coyuacan. He had, in fact, at one stroke moved up the southern causeways to within easy striking distance of Mexico without having to force a passage yard by yard, as he had thought at first would be necessary.

Olid and part of his force joined Cortés at the junction, leaving Coyuacan strongly held; and Sandoval also moved up. Meanwhile Alvarado was trying to advance along the Tacuba causeway. Cortés sent him six sloops to protect his flanks. The general plan was to co-ordinate the advances along the southern and western causeways until both forces met in the centre of the city.

But though Cortés had made so rapid a start, he made little progress during the next fortnight. On June 9th Sandoval and his men were transferred from the Iztapalapan causeway to the northern causeway at Tepeyacac, an essential move as the Mexicans were using it as a supply route. His orders were the same as Alvarado's—to force his way in and meet the others in the city. In spite of the protection given by the sloops, breaches in the causeways made it very difficult to advance. The Mexicans turned the breaches into fortified points, with barricades on their side and stakes in the water. In some places there were reeds in which canoes were hidden and from which they sallied unexpectedly. It was impossible to prevent them from bringing in provisions, as the sloops could not be everywhere at once. On two occasions Cortés succeeded in raiding the city and even penetrated as far as the great temple opposite his old quarters in Lord Face of Water's palace. But he was unable to maintain himself in this advanced position. He managed to set fire to some of the houses in the main square, including Montezuma's palace, and the zoo, but was driven back to his original position on the causeway. The breaches, which he had filled up with rubble on his way, were reoccupied by the Mexicans and the filling removed. It seems that a portable bridge was impracticable because the breaches varied greatly in width.

Alvarado made even less progress on the Tacuba causeway. Bernal gives a detailed description of the struggle there. They fought all day long and sometimes at night. On June 23rd they suffered a serious reverse. The Mexicans pretended to retreat. The Spaniards pursued and crossed a wide breach by wading through the water which in this case was not very deep. Cortés had ordered that all breaches were to be filled before advancing beyond them. Alvarado, in the ardour of pursuit, disobeyed this order. While the retreating Mexicans drew him further along the causeway, another body of them landed from canoes in his rear, occupied the breach, deepened it, and put pointed stakes in pits. The retreating enemy then counter-attacked and drove him back into the breach. A ferocious struggle ensued in which six Spaniards were taken for sacrifice. Bernal has one of his heartfelt entries: 'I swear it was a wonder we were not all killed in the pits. As for myself, I may say that I was laid hold of by several Mexicans but got my arm free and by the grace of Lord Jesus saved myself with some good sword thrusts. But I was badly wounded in one arm. When I got out of the water into safety, I lost consciousness. I could not stand on my feet and had no breath left. I declare that when they had me in their clutches I commended myself to God and his blessed Mother. He gave me the strength to break away. Thank God for the mercy He vouchsafed me.' When Cortés heard of Alvarado's narrow escape from disaster, he was very angry at his disobedience and sent a letter by sloop to warn him never again to advance over a breach without filling it in and posting men to hold it. But as we shall see, the same negligence was to occur in his own division.

In spite of this reverse and the slow progress of the siege, those of the lake towns which had not already sided with Cortés now sent envoys to offer assistance. By joining him they brought the total number of his auxiliaries to 100,000 men. Besides troops, they supplied a quantity of canoes, enough to make it very difficult for the Mexican canoes to bring in supplies. From this date—towards the end of June—the city had little food or water from outside. The lake was salt and few fresh-water wells existed on the island. Had it not been the rainy season with heavy downpours every day, the besieged could hardly have held out.

Cortés thought the moment had arrived for a concerted dash by his divisions. The rendezvous was to be, not the great square, but the market-place in the north-west part of the city. There was room there for all his troops. If he could win it, Lord Falling Eagle would be confined to the north-east corner of the island and the end would be in sight. The attack was fixed for June 30th. Sandoval was ordered to join forces with Alvarado. There were to be two thrusts, not three.

The two divisions began to advance along their respective causeways at dawn. Cortés made rapid progress, entered the city, passed through the great square and reached the entry to the northern city, called Tlatelolco it will be remembered, which was divided from Mexico proper by a canal broader than those which intersected the metropolis elsewhere. Bundles of reeds, maize stalks and wood were hastily flung into it. The vanguard crossed. The market-place was only half a mile away. Victory seemed assured. Sandoval and Alvarado were not far off; the noise of their fire-arms, shouting and trumpets, could be heard.

Suddenly the Mexicans counter-attacked in overwhelming force. The vanguard ran back to the canal. The stuff which had been thrown into it had sufficed to bear the weight of men crossing in good order. It now collapsed and sank under the rush. Again a breach had been left imperfectly filled in the rear. This time the result was far more disastrous.

Cortés had not crossed the breach with the vanguard. He was busy on a flank. Intending to make sure the breach had been filled, he came to inspect it and arrived at the moment when the vanguard was driven back into it. A struggling mass of Spaniards and their auxiliaries was in the water. Mexicans in canoes were taking them prisoner and paddling them away. Cortés, who was on foot, tried to save his men. He writes to the Emperor: 'I determined to remain there and die fighting. The most that I and my company could do was to lend a hand to some unlucky Spaniards who were drowning and help them out. Occupied in this way I did not notice the danger I was in. Some Mexicans grasped me and would have carried me off.' And he describes how Cristobal de Olea, one of his captains, rescued him, though in doing so he himself was killed. Another of his body-guard, exclaiming: 'Without you we are all dead men,' hustled him into safety. A horse was brought. He mounted and managed to control the rout. His division fell back on the main square. The battle continued to rage there. Clouds of incense were observed rising from the platform of the Humming Bird's pyramid. The priests were evidently preparing to sacrifice. The attack became more violent. The Mexicans slung some heads at the Spaniards. The cry was that one of the heads was Alvarado's. After suffering great loss, estimated at sixty-six Spaniards taken alive, others killed and wounded badly, seven horses killed and many crossbows, muskets and one cannon lost, Cortés' division reached its fortified camp on the causeway.

Bernal tells us what happened on the west side where Alvarado was attacking. All seemed going well and they expected shortly to reach the Tlatelolco market, when suddenly 'we saw advancing against us with loud yells a large body of Mexicans, men of rank with handsome ensigns and plumes. They threw in front of us five heads streaming with blood. "As you can see," they cried, "here are the heads of Cortés and Sandoval. You all will soon share their fate." ' They attacked so violently that the Spaniards were driven out of the city. As they retreated on to the Tacuba causeway they heard the horn of Falling Eagle. 'This horn was sounded as a signal that his captains and soldiers must fight to capture their enemies or die in the attempt. When the sound of it echoed in their ears, the fury and courage with which they threw themselves on us to catch hold of our bodies was terrifying and I do not know how to describe it here. Even now as I stop to remember, it is as though I could see it all at this minute.'

When half-way down the causeway, the Spaniards heard the dismal booming of the drum of snake-skin which stood on the top of the great pyramid in the square. There was also a clamour of horns, conch shells and trumpets. 'We all looked towards the lofty temple where they were being sounded and saw that our comrades whom they had captured when they defeated Cortés were being carried by force up the steps. They were taking them to be sacrificed. When they got them on to the platform before the shrine, we saw them stick plumes on the heads of many of them. They made them dance before the Humming Bird with what looked like fans in their hands. After they had danced they immediately placed them on their backs on the sacrificial stones and with stone knives they sawed open their chests, drew out their palpitating hearts, and offered them to the idols. They kicked the bodies down the steps. Butchers waiting below cut off the arms and feet and flayed the faces. The trunks they threw to the carnivora.' The memory of the terrible scene leads Bernal to add: 'Now that I am far away from the hard battles of those days, I want to explain the feeling I had after seeing these horrors. It was dread that one day or another they would do the same to me. Afterwards I used to feel terrified before going into battle. But it always happened that once in the battle, I forgot my fear.'

Bernal was brave enough not to be ashamed of admitting his

fear, and simple enough not to be aware of his vanity. Of all the conquistadores he is the one we know best. What a wonderful old face he must have had when in his seventy-sixth year he completed his chronicle. He tells us he wrote it that truth should prevail. A history of the conquest was published in 1553 by Gómara, a writer who was Cortés' chaplain in Spain in the fifteen-forties. He got his information from Cortés himself and other conquistadores. Bernal read the history and thought it very inaccurate. This spurred him to write his own *True History of the Conquest*, though he was diffident about his style, which he knew had no resemblance to the literary style of the period. To-day, Gómara is unreadable, while Bernal, though his narrative would have greatly benefited by severe pruning, is mostly fresh and delightful. He is the interesting case of a natural artist—a Douanier Rousseau of the pen. His book was finished in 1568. When he died in 1581 at the age of eighty-nine it had not yet been published. Not till 1632 did it appear in print. In a last analysis he has secured immortality for two reasons—he wrote the truth and he was never dull. Not the least extraordinary fact about the drama of Cortés and Montezuma is that one of its eye-witnesses was a story-teller of genius.

€26§

Cortés Storms Mexico City

The failure of Cortés' attempt to storm the city on June 30th encouraged the Mexicans and discouraged the auxiliaries. The Mexicans thought that at last they had got their magic calculations right. Moreover, about this time they received a direct message from the Humming Bird through their priest mediums. In their trance these declared in the curious twittering voice associated with the Humming Bird's oracles that within eight days the Spaniards would be destroyed. This utterance was no doubt found to conform with deductions made under the complicated system of correspondences which conditioned Mexican augury. Falling Eagle considered that he had as sound reasons for believing it as it was possible to have. Students of Mexican lore have attempted to indicate the precise reasons, and their surmises are worth recording because they help to illustrate the curious nature of Mexican thought. Quetzalcoatl had, among several forms, that of the planet Venus. Every 584 days Venus is in conjunction with the sun, when, as the Evening Star, it disappears immediately after sunset. This period of invisibility lasts eight days. It was believed that Venus-Quetzalcoatl lost his heavenly power during these eight days. He was swallowed by the earth; as the Mexicans saw it, he was in the jaws of the grave. Since he was at his weakest, it was the right moment to attack him. It has been calculated that Venus was in conjunction in July-August 1521. One can be sure that the oracle which pronounced Cortés' coming destruction was founded on that astronomical fact. Interesting to record, if you work back 584 days from August 1521, you get December 1519, which was the date which Lord Maize Cobs fixed as propitious for the rising which Cortés anticipated by arresting him. It should be added that in the normal way it was only at these eight-day periods of weakness that human sacrifices were made to Quetzalcoatl, probably on the ground that he must have human hearts to revive him.

When the auxiliaries heard of the oracle, they also believed it. Hitherto they had put their faith in the old prophecy that that Smoking Mirror was fated to go down before Quetzalcoatl. But the oracle shook their faith. Nearly all of them deserted Cortés. The auxiliary army of 100,000 was suddenly reduced to a couple of hundred or so.

During the ensuing week the most that Cortés could do was to maintain the siege by remaining on the causeways and sweeping the lake with his sloops. He was encouraged by the news that provisions were running short in the city and the water in its improvised wells was brackish. The Mexicans attacked violently down the causeways, but as they had always to make a frontal attack against muskets and cannon, it was possible to keep them at bay. The fire-arms taken in the rout they did not attempt to use, though they discharged a few arrows from captured crossbows.

When the eight days were up and the Spaniards had not been wiped out, the auxiliaries began to return to Cortés' standard. Evidently ancient prophecy was right. Smoking Mirror had been unable to prevail, even at the moment when Quetzalcoatl was at his weakest. Now, as the Morning Star, he was in full power again. Cortés regained all his ascendancy over the minds of his allies. They sent even more troops than before. Moreover, a ship with powder and arms put into Vera Cruz at this time, a great piece of luck as powder was very low.

Another attempt was now made to induce Falling Eagle to surrender. He was offered good terms. Cortés promised not only to spare his life, but to retain him as vassal ruler. Refusal to make peace would inevitably result in the destruction of the city and the death of its inhabitants. Bernal says Falling Eagle said to his advisers: 'I have already tried everything I can do and have changed my manner of fighting several times, but the Spaniards are of such a nature that when we thought that we held them conquered, they turned the more vigorously against us.' This sentence (a good example of how Bernal had an intuitive insight into the Mexican mind, though he did not fully understand it) implies, in addition to its obvious meaning, that Falling Eagle had never doubted the supernatural quality of his assailants. He had used every magical device known to him, particularly sacrifice, but they had counter devices of greater potency, which could not be provided against because it was not known how they worked.

The other members of the Mexican council were against Cortés' offer. They had come to think that, whatever they did, ruin was certain. They were doomed. Better then go down fighting. Falling Eagle accepted their advice.

From this onwards, Cortés determined on a methodical reduction of the city. He would not again make a dash for the market, but would advance up the causeways, enter the streets, destroy the houses one by one, use their materials to fill the canals where bridges had been, and so make the city safe to manœuvre in with cavalry and artillery.

By July 25th he had taken the southern part as far as the main square and on July 28th Alvarado, coming in on the west, met him in the market-place of Tlatelolco. On the way Bernal went into a shrine and saw on poles 'many of the heads of our Spaniards whom they had sacrificed. Their hair and beards had grown much longer than when they were alive. I would not have believed it, had I not seen it.'

By the market-place was Smoking Mirror's large pyramid

which they had visited eighteen months earlier on their first coming to Mexico. Cortés set fire to it, after destroying its images. This act recalled what the apparition of Smoking Mirror had said to Montezuma's envoys, when he told them to look back at Mexico and see how its temples were in flames.

The Mexicans were now confined to the north-east corner of the city. This was mostly a lake sector; a great part of the buildings stood on piles in the water. The population had been pressed back into this area which contained about a thousand houses. The number of people who lived in Mexico is not exactly known and estimates vary between a third and two-thirds of a million. Allowing that some thousands had been killed, had died of privation, had fled or been sent to the mainland, the number left must have been considerable. They were starving. But their spirit was unbroken.

Again Cortés sent proposals for peace. A message came from Falling Eagle that he agreed to a parley. Cortés went, but the other was not there. Instead were two lords, who declared it was unsafe for their master to come. On Cortés attemping to re-assure them, they maintained a sceptical air and, as if to persuade him that they had no lack of food, 'drew from a bag they carried some maize cakes, a leg of turkey and cherries and, seating themselves in a very leisurely manner, began to eat'. The negotiations came to nothing.

The best description of the last stages of the siege is in Cortés' letter to Charles. After relating how the negotiations failed and how he resolved on a combined assault on the north-east corner, his army attacking on the land side and his launches under Sandoval from the lake, he writes: 'Such was the slaughter done on water and on land, that with prisoners taken the enemy's casualties numbered in all more than 40,000 men. The shrieks and weeping of the women and children were so terrible that we felt our hearts breaking. We had more trouble in preventing our auxiliaries from killing and inflicting tortures than we had in fighting. No such inhuman cruelties, as practised by the natives of these parts, were ever seen amongst any people.' He goes on to complain that the auxiliaries, who as they numbered 150,000 could not be controlled by the small Spanish force, took a quantity of plunder, which he would have liked to get. Indeed, one of his reasons for seeking a negotiated surrender was that in an assault the greater part of the wealth of the city would be stolen by the auxiliaries or thrown into the lake by the desperate defenders.

The first day of the final assault ended indecisively. The next morning Cortés managed to have speech with the Mexican Commander-in-Chief, the successor of the Serpent Woman killed at the battle of Otumba. But this officer repeated that Falling Eagle was resolved to fight to the last. 'I told him,' writes Cortés, 'to return to his people, and that he and they might prepare themselves, as I was determined to finish destroying them. More than five hours had passed in these parleyings. The inhabitants of the city were all treading on the dead. Others in the water were swimming and others drowning themselves in the large lake. Such was the plight in which they were that one cannot conceive how they could endure it. An infinite number of men, women and children kept coming towards us, who in their haste pushed one another back into the water and were drowned amidst the multitude of dead. They had already perished to the number of 50,000 from the salt water they drank or from starvation and pestilence. As these people came towards us, I ordered Spaniards to be stationed in all the streets in order to prevent our auxiliaries from killing the unhappy creatures. But as they were so many it was not possible to prevent it that day and more than 15,000 persons were massacred.'

A position was reached when most of the remaining Mexican soldiers were perched on the roofs of the houses which stood in the water of the lake itself. Their position was hopeless. They were separated in small groups; and they had no stones or arrows left or means of procuring a further supply. It was the moment for Sandoval to steer his sloops among the houses and let his musketeers and crossbowmen pick off the defenders on the roofs. Cortés gave him the order. He made straight for the building where Falling Eagle was holding out.

But Falling Eagle, even at this moment of general massacre, when the auxiliaries, once his subjects, seemed bent on a complete extermination of the Mexican people, was not going to surrender. He had with him some fifty canoes. He, his wife, who was Montezuma's daughter, his ladies and his courtiers embarked on them with the intention of escaping to the mainland. He also took on board his personal treasure. When Sandoval arrived he had gone. Sloops were immediately sent in pursuit. A certain García Holquin, who commanded the fastest sailer, overtook the canoes. Among them was one with awnings and a royal seat, evidently Falling Eagle's boat. Holquin signalled to him to stop and, when he did not, threatened to fire. Falling Eagle, seeing that he and his womenfolk were covered by the musketeers, accepted his fate and gave himself up. 'Spare my women,' he said, 'and take me at once to Malintzin.'

'When Holquin heard this,' says Bernal, 'he was greatly delighted and with much respect he embraced him and placed him in the sloop. He gave him mats to sit on and offered him refreshments.' Sandoval soon afterwards arrived in his sloop and demanded the royal prisoner. But Holquin, who expected a great reward, refused to give him up except directly to Cortés.

Cortés had mounted a pyramid in Tlatelolco to watch the pursuit. On seeing the capture of Falling Eagle, he gave orders for a guest chamber to be got ready with hangings and comfortable seats, and a good meal to be prepared. It was not long before Sandoval and Holquin appeared; Falling Eagle was walking between them. Cortés embraced him with animation and spoke warmly to the lords who followed him. But Falling Eagle could not respond to this show of courtly manners. What had happened he saw only as the last scene in a tragedy. He declared: 'My duty is done. I can do no more. I did not surrender. I was taken prisoner by force.' And placing his hand on the dagger which Cortés had in his belt, he said with intense emotion: 'Stab me.' The tears were running down his face. 'Cortés replied affectionately, through Doña Marina,' writes Bernal, 'saying he esteemed him for his bravery, that he attached no blame to him in anything.' One is bound to say that no commander of modern times would conduct himself with such gallant politeness to a fallen enemy who had put all his prisoners to a cruel death. But it was the code of the day for a victor to show a splendid magnanimity to the leader of the other side. The part was easy for Cortés. His grace was natural; excited and relieved by victory, he radiated happiness. Bernal had noticed this characteristic of his at the time of Narváez's defeat. It was with the same gaiety and magnificence that he comforted Falling Eagle. 'When he bade me stab him I encouraged him and told him not to be afraid,' he wrote to Charles. The letter goes on: 'This lord having been made prisoner, the war immediately ceased, which God Our Lord was pleased to bring to its end on this day, the 13th of August 1521, seventy-five days after we first laid siege to the city.'

The end of the fighting was so sudden that the absence of noise seemed very strange. Bernal thought it was like being in a belfry when the bells all at once stop ringing. The soldiers wondered if they were deaf. For so long there had been shouting, the sound of drums and trumpets, of hammering, whistles, conch-shells, cannon. 'At the capture of Falling Eagle the clamour ceased.'

The drama of Cortés and Montezuma had ended in silence.

Postscript

As this book is devoted to an interpretation of what transpired when Cortés and Montezuma were face to face, it comes to a natural conclusion with the fall of Mexico. A postscript is added to give the reader a short summary of subsequent events in the careers of Cortés and his associates.

Cortés' first task was to rebuild the city, which had been almost wholly destroyed. The debris of the old houses and the pyramid temples, which were now pulled down, provided ready material. On the sites of the temples Christian churches were built. A Spanish town came into existence. The surviving Mexicans returned and occupied it. While this was being done, Cortés lived in Coyuacan (The Place of Many Lean Coyotes). Falling Eagle stayed with him. One of the first questions asked was where Montezuma's treasure had been hidden. The bulk of it was captured from the Spaniards, as will be recalled, on the night when they had fled the city. Falling Eagle declared that it had mostly been lost in the ensuing troubles. He was not believed and to make him speak he was tortured. The army insisted on this and Cortés acquiesced. The torture produced some valuables, but not many. However, added to Falling Eagle's personal treasure, which was captured with him, the amount of gold for distribution was considerable. As before, when the fifths had been deducted and the leaders had taken their shares, the rank and file did not get more each than about the cost of a new crossbow.

The end of Mexican sovereignty might have resulted in the numerous vassal towns declaring their independence. Cortés called on them to acknowledge Charles V. They submitted and the political unity of the country was preserved. He also founded several Spanish towns, where his followers were settled and given estates with forced labour. These towns were the centres from which Spanish ideas were spread. European animals were imported, especially cattle and pigs. Cortés began to display administrative talents. He wanted to avoid the errors which had been made in Hispaniola and Cuba, where in a rush to get rich quickly the Spaniards had ruined the West Indies. By treating the local aristocracy as equals he strove to enlist their co-operation in a policy which would assure the welfare of the general population.

While striving to lay the foundations of New Spain on sound economic principles, Cortés sought also to extend its boundaries and ascertain more comprehensively its geographical position. The Spaniards had still only a vague idea where they were. That Mexico was on a comparatively narrow strip of land connecting two vast continents was not yet known. Nor did they know how far the America they had discovered was from China. The news of Magellan's circumnavigation of the world did not reach Spain till August 1522. Cortés became an explorer of Central America and the South Seas.

In October 1522, fourteen months after the fall of Mexico, he received letters from Charles V recognizing his conquest, absolving him from blame for having thrown off Velázquez's authority, and appointing him Governor and Captain-General of New Spain. The Emperor, however, sent out four officials, a Treasurer, an Accountant, a Trade Agent and an Inspector, whose duty was to report to him and look after his interests. Cortés ceased to be an independent ruler and became an official governor within the Spanish administrative system.

Postscript

Early in 1524 the first Friars arrived from Spain. They were sent to convert the country to Christianity. Some of them were very remarkable men, like Sahagún, whose writings on the conquest, notable for their pro-Mexican point of view, have been quoted earlier in this book. But though the Friars stood for justice and fair treatment for the native inhabitants, they favoured the destruction of their art. The temples and sculptures were broken up. The magical treatises, which were the repositories of American thought, were burnt. The art which has survived to this day is what escaped their diligent efforts to obliterate everything which might remind the people of their non-Christian culture. But in destroying the indigenous culture, the Spaniards were not doing more than all European nations did or tried to do, both at that date and later, when they made conquests out of Europe.

The Mexicans and the other races of the country accepted Christianity without difficulty. It does not seem that they changed their first view as to the identity of Cortés with Quetzalcoatl. Christianity therefore had the authority behind it of one of their own gods. Their magical books had foretold its coming and declared that the other gods would go out. Cortés remained the visiting god, a mysterious incomprehensible figure. The new church was the form his teaching took. That he was now one of Charles V's officials was hard to fathom. But their experience was that his actions were always unpredictable, yet that the sum of them amounted to a fulfilment of prophecy. They saw the great state in which he lived at Coyuacan, his immense household with its ceremonial. He seemed to them a dazzling and extraordinary personage, as he did also to the Spaniards, though his countrymen were jealous of his success and disliked his liberal policy, which prevented them from exploiting the country as quickly and savagely as they wished.

That the inhabitants of Central America embraced Christianity, built and decorated churches, became devotees of the

Postscript

Virgin and abandoned human sacrifice is not to say that they lost all belief in the old gods and the old magic. Smoking Mirror, in his two forms as king of the gods and war god, disappeared when the government of which he was an integral part came to an end. The battle had been directly between him and Quetzalcoatl and, as prophesied, he lost it. But there was a legion of minor gods, whose worship was connected with everyday things, such as the crops, disease and the weather. Though the new church did not countenance these gods, though their priesthoods were dissolved and their places of worship dismantled, the people believed them to be still present and to have some residue of power. They were tended in secret and their oracles consulted. As time went on they became a part of legend and folk-lore. They underwent all kinds of transformations. In that world of fancy it was possible for them to become Christian, even to become saints. Some of their images were put into the foundations of churches, some into the walls of granaries. Their story was kept alive in folk dances. Others of them became witches and others fairies. As the centuries passed an inextricable confusion arose. Tepuztecatl, the old god of wine, claimed that he was a son of the Virgin. Mr. Rodney Gallop, who made a stay in Mexico during the nineteen-thirties, tells us in his *Mexican Mosaic* of traces of the ancient beliefs he came across in remote villages. The old gods are still alive. And their numbers have been added to. Near Tlaxcala there is a volcano which in Cortés' time was called Matlalciuatl (the Dark Green Woman). The divine denizen of this mountain was afterwards identified with Doña Marina and the mountain is now called Malinche, her name. Perhaps stranger still is Mr. Gallop's discovery that Montezuma has become a god. He is a god of two aspects. In San Cristóbal he is the Lord of Sickness and has to be exorcized in song; at Cuaxtla he is the giver of good crops and good health.

That Cortés had a wife has been mentioned, a woman called Catalina Xuárez whom he left in Cuba. In June 1522 she arrived unexpectedly in port and came up to Mexico. Three months later she died in somewhat mysterious circumstances. Bernal calls it a 'delicate subject'. Cortés was accused afterwards by his enemies of murdering her and there was an inquiry. He was held blameless. No wife can have contributed less to her husband's greatness than did Catalina.

Cortés cut a tremendous figure in Mexico. Narváez, who had been a prisoner in Vera Cruz all this while, was allowed to come up to the capital. After being taken round to see the sights, he was received by Cortés. Penniless, one eye with a patch over it, and a bit shabby, he was a changed man, as the following extract from Bernal shows: 'When Narváez came before Cortés he fell on his knees and tried to kiss his hands, but Cortés would not allow it, but raised him up and embraced him, showed him much affection and ordered him to take a seat near him.' Cortés, as we know, was always affectionate to fallen enemies. Narváez had a booming sepulchral voice, 'as if he was speaking in a vault', says Bernal, and this mannerism made it all the funnier when he went on to refer to the snub which Cortés had given him at Vera Cruz. 'After seeing the great cities you have conquered, sir, I frankly admit that your defeat of me was indeed the least of what you and your valiant soldiers have accomplished in New Spain. One can place your Excellency, and I do, ahead of all the most famous and illustrious men who have ever lived anywhere.' Later on Narváez was allowed to return to Spain, where he tried all he could to vilify Cortés, but he did himself no good. As I have said, he was a stupid man.

After three years of colonial administration Cortés grew restless. Soon after the conquest he had sent his Captain, Crístobal de Olid, with a fleet to found a town in the region eastward of the Yucatán peninsula, now called Honduras. In due course Olid revolted and declared himself independent. Cortés decided to march on him overland. This meant passing through Guatemala, hitherto unexplored. He was prompted to do this, partly

Postscript

by his taste for campaigning and partly because, touched by a mania for exploring, he hoped to find a sea passage between the Atlantic and the Pacific, which was reputed to exist in or about the longitude of Honduras. He left Mexico in October 1524.

Bernal went with him and his picture of his chief's entourage gives us a glimpse of the magnificent lord that Cortés had become. Though going on a campaign to distant unknown regions, he took with him great services of gold and silver plate, three clerics to preach, a major-domo, a butler, a steward and a chamberlain. He had a doctor and a surgeon, several pages, eight grooms and two falconers. To keep his friends amused in the evening he brought five musicians, good both for wind and strings, an acrobat, a conjurer and a puppet master. Of his old companions he had Sandoval and Doña Marina. He also took Falling Eagle with him.

The expedition to Honduras lasted much longer than Cortés expected. He was absent from Mexico a year and nine months. He did not accomplish anything in particular, but experienced greater hardships and dangers than in all his previous campaigns. Two events are to be mentioned. Doña Marina married and Falling Eagle was hanged. Marina, thriving in troubles as was foretold, had become the most celebrated woman in Mexico. For five years she had been everywhere with Cortés as his interpreter and consort, and was the mother of his son. He now gave her in marriage to a Captain Xaramillo, who had commanded one of his sloops. She continued as interpreter (Aguilar was dead by now, but she had learnt Spanish) and saw the campaign through. It is agreeable to know that she lived to a good age, enjoying a large income from her estates, with a town house in Mexico, a country house in Chapultepec, and in Coyuacan a garden which had belonged to Montezuma. After her death, as we have learned, she became a mountain goddess.

Falling Eagle was hanged because it was alleged that he had conspired with other Mexican lords on the expedition to kill Cortés and head a rising against the Spaniards. There has been much discussion about the justice of this execution. Bernal liked the ex-king personally and thought he was innocent. Cortés believed there was a conspiracy and that he was privy to it. Falling Eagle had been taken on the expedition because it was held unsafe to leave him behind. Though evidently not altogether to be trusted, Cortés had spared him hitherto, partly out of policy and partly because it was his nature to spare the vanquished. One inclines to think that he would not have executed him now without strong grounds. Falling Eagle has become a national hero. But, as I have already suggested, it is doubtful whether such conceptions existed in the days of the astro-magical sovereigns of pre-Cortésian Mexico.

Before he left on the expedition to Honduras Cortés had appointed two of the four royal officials, whom Charles had sent out, to administer the country in his absence. On learning that these two were misbehaving themselves, he sent orders appointing the other two. They were even worse scoundrels and soon Mexico was in confusion. When he had been absent a year and no letters had come from him for many months, they gave out that he was dead, enriched themselves by torturing the Mexican lords and even seized his property. In addition they drew up an indictment against him, accusing him of treason, murder, and robbery, which they forwarded to Spain. On his return to Mexico he got the better of them, but they had done his reputation so much harm with Charles V that he thought it necessary to go to Spain and clear himself.

He left Mexico in March 1528, taking with him one of Montezuma's sons, two of the lords of Tlaxcala, a quantity of gold and jewels, Mexican wild animals and curiosities. In the autumn of the same year he was received by Charles. He had little difficulty in persuading the Emperor that the charges made against him had no foundation. As a reward for his great services he was raised to the peerage with the title of Marquess of the Valley of Oaxaca, in which fertile and beautiful locality he was granted huge estates with feudal powers over 23,000 vassals. He remained Captain-General, but was not confirmed as Governor. Charles decided to make Mexico a viceroyalty and to appoint a Spanish grandee. This was a very great disappointment to Cortés, who not only felt that he had a better right than any other man to rule Mexico, but also had the knowledge, the goodwill and the imagination to make it a model province of the empire.

During his visit to Spain he arranged marriages in the Spanish nobility for daughters of Montezuma, and himself married Doña Juana de Zúñiga, niece of the Duke of Béjar. Sandoval, his closest companion in the conquest, who had come home with him, died, to his great grief. He left for Mexico in the spring of 1530 and landed at Vera Cruz in July.

For the next ten years he lived on his estates and went exploring in the South Sea. He was in eclipse, for the government was conducted by the Viceroy, Don Antonio de Mendoza. Nevertheless, as a great landlord he had some scope for his ideas and administered his estates like a little kingdom. He hoped that the ships he sent into the South Sea would lead to his discovery and conquest of a country as large, perhaps, and rich as Mexico, and which he would be permitted to govern. But one does not conquer a Mexico twice in a lifetime. The Spanish discoveries and conquests in the Pacific, notably of the Philippines, were the work of other men.

In 1540 Cortés left again for home. He was now much less of a figure than in 1530 when fresh from his conquests he had dazzled the Court. Nothing he had done in Mexico during the last ten years was in any way comparable to his former achievements. Moreover, a new conqueror had appeared on the scene. In 1535 Pizarro conquered Peru, whose loot yielded far more gold than Mexico. He, too, was made a Marquess. It was in his deeds, his treasure, that people were interested. Cortés seemed a tiresome figure out of the past, a man whose fame belonged to history, and who had nothing new to tell or give. He was received with civility, but when it was seen that his object in coming home was to complain to the Emperor about this and that, old scores, old debts, old broken promises and unpaid debts, he was slighted, kept waiting, and given no satisfaction. He had become a bore. The Emperor had been told so often that Cortés had won territories for him in the New World larger than those he ruled in the Old. To be told it again was irritating, and by a man, too, who looked older than his years and was unlikely to be of further use. Had he not been amply rewarded with titles and estates? To have to listen to his protests and complaints was unendurable. He was put off with vague promises.

In the following year, 1541, Charles fitted out an expedition against Algiers with the object of breaking the Moslem power in the Mediterranean. A war against the Moors was still regarded as a crusade. The nobility of the empire joined with enthusiasm. The Marquess of the Valley, hoping perhaps to do some deed under the Emperor's eye that would bring him back into favour, was among those who volunteered. He came with his son, Don Martín, born of Doña Marina, and 'many esquires and servants, horses and a great company, in a fine galley'. When the imperial forces were investing Algiers, a violent storm destroyed several ships. Cortés' galley was wrecked. Before abandoning it, says Bernal, 'the servants of Cortés saw him tie in a handkerchief twisted round his arm certain jewels of great value, which he carried as a great lord though to do so was unnecessary display. In the confusion of escaping to safety these precious stones were lost.' They were emeralds of unusual size which had been part of Montezuma's treasure. After the disaster to his fleet, Charles held a council of war, which advised withdrawal. Cortés was not invited to the council but, when he heard of its decision, he offered to undertake the capture of Algiers, if they gave him the command, even if he had for the purpose no more than 400 men, the number which had sufficed him to conquer Mexico. This sounded like the boast of a doting old soldier and was greeted with merriment by the council.

Postscript

Cortés returned from the expedition weary and worn. He continued to hope that Charles would listen to his complaints and perhaps raise him to some high employment. Though he wanted to return to his estates in Mexico, he continued to hang about the Court and to follow Charles on his journeys through the empire. But his health was declining. Before the end he realized that the Emperor would never receive him into his inner Councils, never make him a viceroy, that his career was over, that he should compose his mind. Bernal writes: 'His fever and dysentery continuing and getting worse, he decided to leave Seville and retired to Castilleja de la Cuesta, there to attend to his soul and arrange his will. Our Lord was pleased to take him from this toilsome life on 2nd December 1547.' He was sixty-two years of age. His body was buried in Seville in the chapel of the Duke of Medina Sidonia. Later it was carried to Mexico and reburied in the church of St. Francis in Tetzcuco. In 1629 it was removed to Mexico City and interred in the monastery of St. Francis. But his bones had not yet found their final resting-place, for in 1794 they were transferred to the Hospital of Jesus, which was one of his foundations, and placed in a monumental tomb. Even this was not the end, for in 1823 during the Mexican revolution against the dominion of Spain, a demand was made that they be dug up and burnt. To prevent this the authorities of the Hospital removed them from the tomb and secretly buried them in another part of the church. The spot is unknown, as it was not marked. It is believed that they rest there to-day. But Cortés requires no tomb to perpetuate his memory. He is an historical personage, if ever there was one, of whom the last is far from having been said.

But we must leave him and listen before we close to Bernal as he murmurs the names of the old Conquistadores, a roll-call of the ghosts of his lost companions which brings his long history to its conclusion.

I will begin the list, he says, with Alvarado. I recall so well his winning smile. He was such a handsome man, so frank, such a good horseman, so dashing a fighter. He became Governor of Guatemala and was killed in Jalisco. Sandoval for a while acted as Governor of New Spain and was its Chief Constable. Not very tall but very well made, he was rather bow-legged; his hair was chestnut, as was his beard, and both were curly. He had a little lisp. His horse was the best. But I must stop talking of horses and tell you of de León of Old Castile, of his good shoulders and his generosity. He died on the bridges as we fled from Mexico. De Ordás could not ride a horse. He was Captain of the swordsmen. His face was powerful, his beard black. He was a good talker though he stammered a bit. He died in the affair of Marañon. Then there was Luís Marín, pockmarked, with red beard, and de Ircio, who talked too much. We called him 'Sour Grapes'. He did nothing worthwhile, nor did de Monjaras because he suffered from boils. De Avila was arrogant, de Olea amiable. He it was who saved Cortés at Xochimilco, when the Mexicans had dragged him from his horse 'El Romo', and saved him again in the city, at the cost of his own life. And there was de Tápia, as good on foot as on horseback. Such were our captains, for I have not included those who were in the army of Narváez, Narváez with the long face, echoing voice, red beard, who lost an eye when we defeated him. If I knew how to paint and carve as well as did in my time Michelangelo, I could draw all these captains, so clearly do I remember them. I could even show how each one would enter a battle. Two gentlemen who read my manuscript were astonished at my memory for names and faces. But it is no wonder I remember; we have talked among ourselves so much of old times. I can even remember the rank and file, the Conquistadores who, like myself, were not captains. Alvarado's four brothers, all dead; Sanzedo, so neat we called him the Gallant, who was killed on the bridges; and Maldonado, 'the broad', who died a natural death. And many others, Terrazas, Margiño, de Grado who married a daughter of Montezuma,

Postscript

Hernández, an old man, 'the good old trooper', Caravajal who went deaf, de la Serna, his face scarred, though what became of him has gone out of my head. That reminds me I have forgotten Puertocarrero, who took the golden wheel to His Majesty. I beg him to pardon me the oversight, though he is dead like his companions. Many, many more come back to me, Vendabal's face, as the Mexicans carried him to be sacrificed, Juarez the elder who killed his wife with a grindstone, Goméz one of the few who returned rich to Castile, Enríquez who died of heat-stroke in his armour, de Cieza who hurled the bar so well, Escudero hanged, de Umbria's maimed toes, Mesa drowned, Guzman frozen, Díaz of the clouded eyes, and Portillo who gave away all his riches and became a friar of St. Francis. I, only I, am left, now Magistrate of Santiago of Guatemala. Thank God and our Lord Jesus Christ that I escaped being sacrificed and that, the survivor of so many perils, I have lived to write this memorial.

The Sacrifice of Eight Earthquake

[see overleaf]

Postscript

This picture of human sacrifice is from the *Codex Zouche-Nuttall* in the British Museum. The victim is a Mixtec lord called Eight Earthquake, who in the early part of the eleventh century offered himself as a victim to the gods. He is wearing the paint of the god to whom he offered himself. The priest, who is performing the operation of removing his heart, is shown plunging the sacrificial dagger in his right hand into the breast from which the blood is spouting. The victim is on the sacrificial stone, which is suggested only by his attitude. As he was a volunteer victim he was not held by the arms and legs in the usual way. The sacrifice takes place at the doorway of the shrine on the temple platform. The particular temple is indicated by the little section of roof on the left-hand side, a symbol that it was a temple connected with ceremonial vapour bathing.

Table of Dates

Table of Dates

Table of Dates

October 1522	Cortés receives letter from Charles V recognizing his conquest
October 1524	Cortés' expedition to Guatemala and Honduras
	Execution of Quauhtemoctzin
March 1528	Cortés goes to Spain
May 1530	Cortés returns to Mexico
1535	Conquest of Peru by Pizarro
1540	Cortés again goes to Spain
1541	Cortés at Algiers
2nd December 1547	Death of Cortés in Spain
1568	Bernal Díaz de Castillo finishes his *True History of the Conquest of Mexico*
1581	Death of Bernal Díaz de Castillo
1632	Publication of the *True History of the Conquest of Mexico*

Index

Index

Córdoba, Hernández de: his expedition, 25 seq., 36

Cortés, Hernan, 15, 16; arrives W. Indies, 23; goes to Cuba, 23; his character, 24, 34, 77, 101, 112, 127, 136; his appearance, 34, 35; prepares expedition, 36 seq.; leaves Santiago, 37; at Trinidad and Havana, 38; leaves Cuba, 39; his army, 39; voyage to. Mexico, 40 seq.; fights Tabascoans, 42; meets Marina, 43; lands in Mexico, 47, 60, 61 seq.; receives Montezuma's presents, 66, 67; resolves to march on Mexico city, 68; evades Velázquez's authority, 69 seq.; at Cempoalan, 74 seq.; and Mexican tax collectors, 75; resolves to do impossible, 80; destroys his ships, 80; given fat lord's niece, 81; destroys Totonac gods, 82; marches on Mexico city, 86 seq.; at Tlaxcala, 92; rallies his men, 97, 98; enters Tlaxcala city, 102; enters Cholula, 105; his massacre of Cholulans, 109; invited to Mexico city, 114; first sight of it, 116; entry, 122; first meeting with Montezuma, 123, 124; his beliefs, 127, 136; confines Montezuma, 138 seq.; and Montezuma's treasure, 151; told to go, 163; marches on Narváez, 174 seq.; Mexicans rise against, 178; re-enters Mexico, 181; driven out of Mexico, 193 seq.; at battle of Otumba, 201; reaches Tlaxcala, 203; marches again on Mexico, 210 seq.; narrow escapes in battle, 213; besieges Mexico city, 213 seq.; escapes assassination, 215; counter-attacked, 220; storms Mexico city, 223 seq.; recognized by Charles V, 231; subsequent history, 230 seq.; death and burials, 239

Coyuacan (Place of Many Lean Coyotes), 122, 215, 230

Cozumel, 30, 40

Cuba, 21, 23, 29, 68, 96, 177

Cuitlahuac (Place of the Dunged Water), 121

Cuitlahuac, Lord, 122, 123, 184, 186, 188; death of, 207

Cuitlalpitoc (Big Bellied), 62, 63, 67, 68

Darien (Panama), 22, 40

Durer, 73

Egon, N., 17

Escalante, Juan de, 38, 71, 81, 84, 116; death of, 139

Estrada, Maria de, 197

Falling Eagle, Lord (Quauhtemoctzin), 184, 207, 213, 219, 225, 226; surrenders, 228, 229; tortured, 230; hanged, 235

fat lord (chief of Totonacs), 74, 81, 82, 103, 115, 172

Ferdinand, 21, 30

Francisca, Doña, 150

Gama, Vasco de, 191

Grijalva, Juan de, his expedition, 29 seq.; 35. 36, 57, 58, 59, 61

Guatemala, 234

Hispaniola, 21, 22, 34, 35

Holquin, García, 228

Honduras, 234

horses, 36, 39, 49, 58, 62, 89, 122

Human Sacrifice, 31, 40, 51 seq., 64, 65, 81, 90, 103, 111, 134, 137, 151, 152, 159, 199, 214, 221, 225

Humming Bird on the Left (Uitzilopochtli), 54, 57, 115; temple of, 125, 133 seq.; great sacrifice to, 137; his main temple, 153 seq.; 199

Index

Index

Index

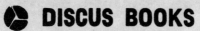

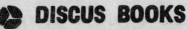

DISCUS BOOKS

DISTINGUISHED NON-FICTION